TRANSFORM YOUR 6-12 MATH CLASS

Digital Age Tools to Spark Learning

AMANDA THOMAS

International Society for Technology in Education
PORTLAND, OREGON • ARLINGTON, VIRGINIA

Transform Your 6–12 Math Class
Digital Age Tools to Spark Learning
Amanda Thomas

Editor: *Emily Reed*
Copy Editor: *Camille Cole*
Proofreader: *Lynda Gansel*
Indexer: *Valerie Haynes Perry*
Book Design and Production: *Kim McGovern*
Cover Design: *Edwin Ouellette*

Library of Congress Cataloging-in-Publication Data available

First Edition
ISBN: 978-1-56484-806-2
Ebook version available.

Printed in the United States of America

ISTE® is a registered trademark of the International Society for Technology in Education.

About ISTE

The International Society for Technology in Education (ISTE) is a nonprofit organization that works with the global education community to accelerate the use of technology to solve tough problems and inspire innovation. Our worldwide network believes in the potential technology holds to transform teaching and learning.

ISTE sets a bold vision for education transformation through the ISTE Standards, a framework for students, educators, administrators, coaches and computer science educators to rethink education and create innovative learning environments. ISTE hosts the annual ISTE Conference & Expo, one of the world's most influential edtech events. The organization's professional learning offerings include online courses, professional networks, year-round academies, peer-reviewed journals and other publications. ISTE is also the leading publisher of books focused on technology in education. For more information or to become an ISTE member, visit iste.org. Subscribe to ISTE's YouTube channel and connect with ISTE on Twitter, Facebook and LinkedIn.

Also by the Author

Transform Your K–5 Math Class: Digital Tools to Spark Learning

Related ISTE Titles

Rev Up Robotics: Real-World Computational Thinking in the K–8 Classroom, by Jorge Valenzuela

About the Author

Amanda Thomas, Ph.D., is an assistant professor of mathematics education in the Department of Teaching, Learning and Teacher Education at University of Nebraska–Lincoln. She received her doctoral degree in 2013 from the University of Missouri–Columbia. Her research focuses on teachers' use of mobile technology in elementary math classrooms. She's also interested in STEM education and supporting teachers in innovative STEM integration.

Acknowledgments

This book was shaped by countless influences, interactions, and individuals who contributed to my vision for math teachers' strategic use of technology in the classroom. Although the cases in the book are fictitious approximations of practice, they were inspired by the practices and challenges shared by countless classroom teachers, preservice teachers, and students over the course of many years. I am grateful for their collective inspiration and insight.

I am also appreciative of my friend and colleague, A.J. Edson, without whom this book would not exist. Our long-term collaboration around technology and mathematics education—and A.J.'s early involvement in the proposal and visioning stages—helped bring this project to fruition. My colleagues and students at the University of Nebraska, Lincoln provide ongoing support for my work. In particular, I thank Lorraine Males for her friendship and guidance, Guy Trainin and Al Steckelberg for their mentorship, Kara Viesca for her insights about book authorship, and Kelley Buchheister for her feedback throughout the writing process and her all-around camaraderie.

This book draws upon the prior work of researchers in technology and math education and I am thankful for the opportunity to build on their work with the support of ISTE and the editors with whom I have worked. I am grateful to Valerie Witte who initiated this project and provided guidance throughout the process, and Emily Reed whose support and feedback led to a finished product that I hope will be useful for technology and math educators.

Dedication

For my family. I dedicate this book to my husband, Michael and adult children, Lexi and Quinton, who have been on this journey with me for decades, and to Leighton and Renden who I hope will enjoy the kinds of math learning experiences envisioned in this book.

Contents

INTRODUCTION

Digital tools open new horizons for learning math. Can math be taught effectively without technology? Sure, it has been for centuries. Can we reasonably expect digital tools to transform a classroom where math is narrowly defined and taught in ways that are inequitable or ineffective? Research and practice tell us no. The question, then, is how can digital tools be integrated in a way that adds value to math classes? When combined with effective teaching practices and interesting, rigorous math content, technology can be a transformative force in the classroom.

This book promotes a vision and path toward transformative use of digital tools to spark learning in secondary (6–12) math classrooms. This book begins with a series of instead of ..., what if... contrasts to spark the imagination about what technology could do in math classrooms. Chapter one explores relevant context, standards, considerations, and challenges. Chapters two through six feature cases and vignettes of technology use in elementary math classrooms. These chapters also provide prompts for reflection and discussion, and connections with research. Chapter seven summarizes the big ideas explored throughout the various classroom cases.

During the course of this book, technology is defined broadly. Some cases highlight math-specific technologies. Others focus on generalized digital tools being used strategically to support math teaching and learning. This book is not a "how to" manual for any particular technologies. Many valuable publications of that nature already exist. Instead, it is an opportunity to think about how a variety of digital tools could be used effectively to teach math in the 6–12 classroom. The cases and vignettes feature a spectrum of technology availability, from a single-teacher device used to facilitate math discussions, to shared devices and 1:1 student technologies. As you read this book, think about the technology tools that are highlighted, the math and teaching practices they support, and how you might implement or adapt these for your own context.

Connecting Classroom Practice with Research

The goal of this book is to bridge research and practice regarding educational technology and math teaching and learning, as illustrated in Figure 0.1.

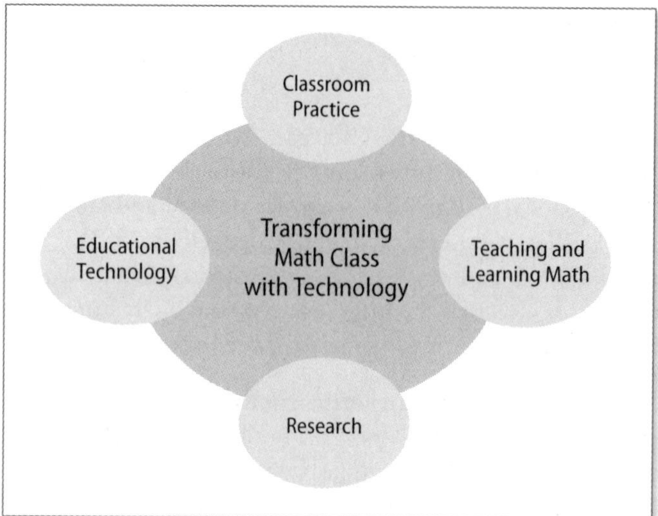

Figure 0.1 Bridging research and practice in math and technology.

By combining what we've learned from research on the subject of best practices in the applications of educational technology in teaching math in 6–12 grade levels, we can begin to develop transformative, technology-rich teaching and learning experiences. We can consider technology and math standards that are based on research and impact practice.

Instead of ..., What if ...?

Oxford Dictionaries defines *transformative* as "causing a marked change in someone or something." When implementing digital tools to transform elementary math classrooms, we consider the status quo and possibilities for marked changes. Perceived barriers to transformation are also considered, including required curriculum, access to technology, and time needed to learn how to use the technology tools. Of course, there are wide variations in the status quo among classrooms, so this book considers a series of *instead of..., what if...* scenarios that contrast frequently-seen uses of technology with bolder possibilities. In these scenarios, we combine a variety of digital tools with best practices for teaching math. These contrasting scenarios include:

- Instead of technology used as a gimmick for "tricking" students into learning math, what if technology was used as an instructional tool to enhance learning of rich math content?

- Instead of using screens for disconnected, individualized learning, what if technology enabled mathematical discourse and collaboration?

- Instead of using technology to assess what students don't know about math, what if we used technology to understand and build upon what students do know?

- Instead of teacher-centered instruction that includes technology, what if we leveraged the interactivity powers of technology to empower student-driven learning?

- Instead of technology for its own sake, what if we used technology in the service of teaching and learning rich, interesting math?

Chapters two through six each begin with contrasting cases that suggest how technology could be transformative in a 6–12 math class. One case describes what often is, and another illustrates what could be[1]. The comparisons are not meant to be critical or evaluative of established practice, but rather the intent is to present alternatives for educators who want to combine innovative technology use with effective math teaching practices. Nevertheless, transformative cases are still imperfect. You may think of more innovative or transformative uses of technology for similar topics; or, the ideas presented in these cases may be replaced by new possibilities enabled by future tools and technologies. These are meant to prompt thought and discussion about how technology can combine with effective math teaching—the primary purpose of these contrasting cases.

You will find reflection and discussion prompts for each of the cases. If you're reading this book on your own, take a moment to think about how the cases presented relate to your own practice and to the big ideas in this book. If you're reading as part of a book club or professional development experience involving other teachers, consider using the prompts to discuss and unpack the important aspects of each case.

Once you've had a chance to read and reflect on the contrasting cases, you'll find that each chapter highlights what current research has to say about those topics. Each chapter concludes with a summary and recommendations for classroom practice as well as alignment with math content and practice standards and ISTE Standards for students and educators. You may find it meaningful to consider how the cases align with standards in your state. If you are reading this book as part of a professional development program, it may be a useful exercise to begin by aligning the cases with relevant standards, and then comparing your alignment with what the author has proposed at the end of each chapter. Whether you are reading this book individually, for your own interest, or with others as part of a professional development experience, take the opportunity to compare each case with your own technology use and math teaching practices. Consider what is and what could be in your own classroom!

1   All individuals and situations in case vignettes are fictional and represent a synthesis of the author's observations and experience in math classroom settings.

CONSIDERATIONS AND CHALLENGES FOR INTEGRATING TECHNOLOGY IN MATH TEACHING

How technology is integrated into one's teaching practices is connected to the models of teaching and approaches to learning that are employed.

THIS CHAPTER INCLUDES overviews of relevant considerations and challenges for integrating digital tools into math instruction in Grades 6–12. These considerations and challenges include a working definition for school math as a socially-constructed endeavor, including equity and access to cutting-edge technology, 1:1 technology initiatives, curriculum resources, and personalized learning. The chapter concludes with a discussion of standards that frame technology and math in secondary classrooms.

What Is School Math?

To many, math is a set of numbers, symbols, formulas, and rules. Others might think of school math in terms of subtopics such as arithmetic, geometry, algebra, and statistics. Mathematicians tend to focus on such things as patterns, structure, logic, proof, modeling, and abstractions. Math content standards have defined specific math learning expectations, as well as standards for math practice that articulate mathematical ways of thinking.

This book draws upon the National Research Council's conception of mathematical proficiency as described in the 2001 book, *Adding it Up: Helping Children Learn Mathematics*. This vision of learning math consists of five interwoven, interdependent threads: conceptual understanding, procedural fluency, strategic competence, adaptive reasoning, and productive disposition. Success in school math has often overemphasized procedural fluency; hence the interpretation of math as numbers, symbols, formulas, and rules. Although being fluent with procedures and algorithms is important, so too are understanding the underlying concepts and connections, formulating problems and choosing useful strategies to solve them, justifying and adapting logical reasoning, and approaching math as a subject worth learning. Technology can and should support all strands of math proficiency, but a quick glance at the market for math apps reveals an abundance of drill and practice applications that emphasize procedural fluency. There are far fewer apps that help develop other strands of proficiency. Although a drill and practice app might be easy to pick up and play, many of the apps that support deeper reasoning and conceptual understanding are most valuable in combination with interesting math problems. Considering all strands of math proficiency can help you, the teacher, make more effective technology choices for your students' learning needs.

Math Learning Is a Socially Constructed Endeavor

When we interpret math proficiency as a combination of procedures, concepts, strategies, reasoning, and disposition, developing math proficiency becomes more complex than numerical problems with multiple choice answers. Traditional models of teaching math have included teacher-centered classrooms where students sat in rows of desks, listened and watched dutifully as the teacher demonstrated how to carry out a procedure, practiced the procedure with the teacher as a class, and then completed independent practice exercises that mimicked what the teacher modeled. This paradigm of instruction is sometimes referred to as *gradual release*, or *I do, We do, You do,* and tends to align with behavioristic transmission of knowledge from teacher to student.

More contemporary models of math teaching center students in their own learning and emphasize procedural fluency in connection with other strands of math proficiency. Rather than asking students to reproduce a demonstration done on the board, teachers monitor and support students as they grapple with challenging math tasks. Facilitating classroom discussions that elicit students' ideas and reasoning builds shared knowledge of concepts, strategies, and procedures. Partner and group work allow students to communicate mathematically and strengthen individual understanding through peer interactions. This model of teaching often employs a *reverse gradual release,* or *You do, We do, I do,* and facilitates classroom interactions that are more consistent with constructivist or sociocultural theories of learning that emphasize active learning in social contexts. How technology is integrated into one's teaching practices is connected to the models of teaching and approaches to learning that are employed.

Equity and Access to Technology and Math

It is not enough for some, or even most students to learn meaningful math and to have access to educational technology. Patterns of inequities disproportionately impact girls, children with special needs, and students from racially, ethnically, and linguistically diverse backgrounds, depriving them of rich learning opportunities. For example, diverse students tend to be overrepresented in "low" math tracks where they are too often met with low expectations and procedurally focused math that is not built on a foundation of conceptual understanding. Here, too, there are often fewer resources and less-experienced teachers.

Likewise, students often do not have equitable access to technology resources and technology-rich learning activities. Achievement gaps on national and international assessments, patterns of enrollment in remedial college math courses, and interest in STEM majors and careers, provide further evidence of these inequities. When considering how to integrate technology into math teaching and learning, it's not enough for *some* students to have access to tools and practices that can transform learning. Instruction should be designed so that each and every student has an opportunity to engage, participate, and develop a positive identity as a math learner.

1:1 Technology Initiatives

Student access to technology devices can be a major barrier for technology integration in math, or any subject. Many schools have been gradually transitioning from dedicated rooms for computer labs to mobile computer/tablet carts, and other options. Recently, we're seeing more 1:1 devices for each student. In some cases, students are issued their own laptop or tablet for an entire school year, or across multiple years. Other options include 1:1 computers that are kept in classrooms for use when teachers and students choose to use them, which is seemingly more common in elementary classrooms. Bring-your-own device (BYOD) initiatives encourage each student to bring their personal computer, tablet, or smartphone. BYOD devices that differ from student to student introduce new challenges for you, the teacher, who must plan across platforms. Overall, ubiquitous access to devices could expand the possibilities for what you and your students could accomplish.

Curriculum Resources

The widespread availability of online open educational resources (OERs) offers a number of advantages for schools, teachers, and students. Especially for schools already investing in 1:1 technologies, free OERs offer significant cost savings over printed textbooks and curriculum materials. Many OERs are customizable for teachers, so you can sequence, add, or omit online content to meet your instructional goals. For students, an obvious benefit of online curriculum resources is convenience. Instead of remembering and transporting multiple books, one digital device can house a wealth of resources. In addition to providing online resources, digital platforms enable teachers, or groups of teachers, to create their own curriculum resources. Digital instructional materials and OERs could democratize access to the creation, customization, and consumption of curriculum. But it's important to note that you, the teacher, must also become a careful curator and cautious consumer of online curriculum resources. In math, for example, comprehensive, coherent, standards-aligned, research-based curriculum materials require many years and a wealth of expertise to develop. Furthermore, free resources often do not go through the same vetting processes as traditionally-published materials.

Personalized Learning

The ISTE Standards for Educators specify that to personalize learning experiences, one should "Capitalize on technology's efficiencies and functionality to meet students' individual learning needs." Few would argue the value of this goal, which sounds a lot like using technology to differentiate instruction. A related idea, sometimes used synonymously with "personalized learning," is "individualized learning." Individual learning programs allow learners to progress through lessons and complete assessments at their own pace. For more than half a century, individualized learning has been tried in classrooms with and without digital technologies. Some of these early individualized learning efforts were called programmed instruction, a term coined by the well-known behaviorist, B.F. Skinner. Modern, technology-based individualized instruction programs may include adaptive assessment, multimedia content, and voluminous data points.

One must question whether or not they are substantively different from programmed instruction. When personalized learning manifests as programmed instruction, teachers must grapple with managing dozens of students, each working on different material at different times, and subject matter becomes reduced to a series of skills-based inputs and outputs. This is hardly the conceptually rich, inquiry-based, authentic learning that you wish to promote. On the other hand, you can and should use technology to create, adapt, and personalize learning experiences in ways that meet students' diverse needs and identities.

Cutting-Edge Technologies

Coding tools, robots, drones, AI, 3D printers: new technologies present new opportunities! Embracing cutting-edge tools can be exciting and valuable for both you and your students. As some early adopters and innovative educators jump at the chance to incorporate the latest technologies, many have wrestled with how new tools could fit in with existing practices, curriculum, and standards. In addition to practical constraints of time, planning, and access to cutting-edge devices, other factors that impact teaching with new technologies include beliefs, knowledge, and attitudes about technology. Additional variables include subject matter and teaching methodologies. To realize the potential of innovative technologies for teaching and learning math, support is required when first learning how to incorporate new tools in combination with effective teaching practices.

Standards for Technology and Math

Technology integration and math teaching are guided and influenced by a variety of standards. The ISTE Standards for Students, Educators, Education Leaders, and Coaches (iste.org/standards) provide a framework for digital age learning across all

TECHNOLOGY AND MATH STANDARDS

ISTE Standards

iste.org/standards

Common Core State Standards for Mathematics

corestandards.org/Math

NCTM Principles to Actions

nctm.org/PtA

Standards for Preparing Teachers of Mathematics

amte.net/standards

disciplines. In math, the Common Core State Standards for Mathematics (corestandards.org/Math) have been adopted in 47 U.S. states and territories since 2010. In 2014, the National Council of Teachers of Mathematics (NCTM) released Principles to Actions: Ensuring Mathematical Success for All. These cross-cutting principles and effective teaching practices are helpful for implementing rigorous math standards (nctm.org/PtA). The Standards for Preparing Teachers of Mathematics (amte.net/standards), released in 2017 by the Association of Mathematics Teacher Educators (AMTE), describe a vision for math teachers. State- and district-level standards for technology and math add another layer of guidelines and expectations for math teachers.

The influence of professional standards for technology and math education extends back nearly three decades. The 1989 Curriculum and Evaluation Standards for School Mathematics, 2000 Principles and Standards for School Mathematics, and 2006 Curriculum Focal Points—all from NCTM— help to provide a coherent, research-informed framework for math teaching and learning that is reflected in many state standards, math textbooks, and teacher preparation and professional development programs. Likewise, the National Education Technology Standards, introduced in 1998, helped to define the technology skills students need to develop. Subsequent standards for teachers (2000) and administrators (2001) articulated ways that stakeholders could support students' development of technology standards. In addition to providing professional recommendations and shaping educational policies, technology and math standards impact curriculum, teacher preparation, and professional development.

Although the standards for technology and math are largely separate realms, they do provide some guidance for integrating math and technology. Many of the ISTE standards cut across content areas, and their recent emphasis on computational thinking relates closely to expectations for teaching and learning math. The Common Core Standards for Mathematical Practice include an expectation that students *use appropriate tools strategically*, and specifically identifies how technologies can support school math instruction. NCTM includes technology among their cross-cutting principles, and AMTE standards include the competency *C.1.6., Use Mathematical Tools and Technology*. The intersection of priorities for teaching and learning math and technology are found in the standards and in recent STEM initiatives (in which technology and math account for half of the STEM acronym). Goals for technology and math teaching and learning have been established by a variety of stakeholders, but you, the teachers, are the ones who bring these goals to life in the classroom.

Considerations and challenges relevant to educational technology and math education frame this book's vision of technology-rich math teaching and learning. Of course, broader considerations and challenges can also impact technology integration. Issues such as quality professional development for teachers, school climate, technology support, teachers' knowledge and beliefs about technology and math, budget constraints for technology, and time constraints are beyond the scope of this book, but nevertheless important for teachers and stakeholders.

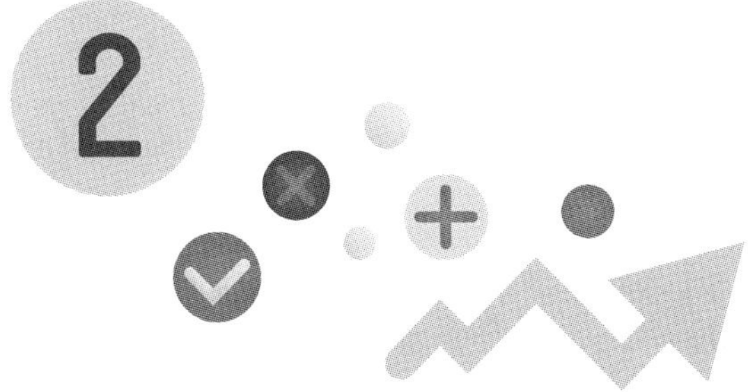

MOVING FROM GIMMICKS
TO TOOLS FOR TEACHING RICH MATH

- Instead of using technology as a gimmick to "trick" students into
- learning math, what if technology is used as an instructional tool
- to enhance the learning of rich math concepts?

IN THIS CHAPTER, you will find two contrasting cases that illustrate teaching eighth-grade binomial multiplication with technology tools. As you read each of the following cases, consider how and what math is being taught, how technology is being used, and how those two ideas connect. After reading and reflecting upon the two contrasting cases, compare your insights and connections with what research has to say about two big ideas illustrated in the cases: *Technology as a Motivational Tool* and *Teaching Practices that Support Mathematical Learning*. Also take a moment to examine how each of the lessons aligns with standards for math content and mathl practices, and ISTE Standards for students, educators, and coaches. Standards alignment is offered at the end of the chapter for your reference.

Technology as a Motivational Tool

It is often accepted as truth that many students love technology. We see evidence of this when they play computer games, spend hours on their phones and tablets, or engage on social media. Although this may not hold true for all students, it is common to use technology as a motivator to capture students' attention, encourage positive behavior, or provide a context for learning that many students might enjoy. When integrating technology into the teaching of a math lesson, look for ways to get students excited about content they sometimes struggle with or dislike. Although it is true that interesting contexts and approaches to learning math can include or be facilitated by technology, we argue that technology can be used as more than a gimmick or an add-on. Effective integration of technology in a math lesson starts with rich content and effective math teaching practices. Technology then becomes a tool to enhance the teaching and learning of math, rather than a distraction or a trick that often does not align with what research tells us about technology and its relationship with teaching and learning math.

Teaching Practices that Support Math Learning

Doing math is more than carrying out algorithms. Teaching practices that support mathlearning must develop fluency by drawing upon students' conceptual understanding, offering opportunities for making connections among multiple representations and strategies, and making student thinking visible. Math teaching that rushes toward fluency without a foundation of conceptual understanding and number sense can be counterproductive. As you look for opportunities to integrate technology into math teaching, it is important that technology use supports what research tells us about how young people learn math.

The following cases demonstrate different approaches to teaching with technology in the math classroom. Questions for reflection and discussion after each of the cases help examine what is working in the lesson and what could be done differently.

 **CASE 2.1**

Ms. Parks's Grade 8 Algebra Lesson

OBJECTIVES

* Multiply binomials using the FOIL method.

Ms. Parks has a cart of laptops in her eighth-grade classroom. Today she is teaching a lesson on multiplying binomials using what she calls the FOIL method. From past years, she knows that many students struggle with this topic. She also knows that many of this year's students seem to enjoy incorporating the laptops during class.

To start her lesson, she announces that students can work on the laptops when they finish their work without any disruptions. She then poses three warm-up problems:

$$x(2x+3) = \underline{\quad} \qquad n(n-4) = \underline{\quad} \qquad (x+1)(x+2) = \underline{\quad}$$

She notices that many students are struggling with the third problem, as anticipated. She gives them two more minutes to finish, and then asks them to compare their answers with someone sitting next to them. She notices that Louise has done the third problem correctly, so after students exchange their answers, Ms. Parks invites her to the board to show the class how she solved $(x+1)(x+2) = \underline{\quad}$. Louise rewrites the problem and shows how she solved the problem. Her work is shown below in Figure 2.1.

Ms. Parks points to Louise's work as she explains the steps she used to multiply, labelling each step as: First–Outside–Inside–Last. She then uses the projector to display four more binomial multiplication problems from a prepared slide on her computer. She slowly shows students how to solve the four problems, explaining each step of the FOIL method, asking questions such as: "What's next?" and "Which ones do we multiply for the Outside step?" These are meant to invite students to participate. After each problem, she asks students if they have any questions, and addresses questions by re-explaining the step that seems to confuse them.

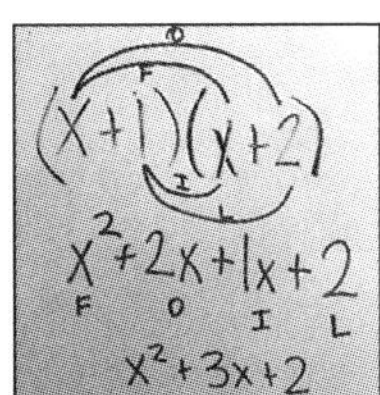

Figure 2.1 Louise's multiplication of *(x+1)(x+2)*

After showing and explaining how to solve the binomial multiplication problems, Ms. Parks assigns ten binomial multiplication problems from the math textbook. She asks all students to solve the problems and then check their answers in the back of the book. Once they finish the problems, they may get a laptop from the cart, go to IXL, and find the Multiply Two Binomials topic. Students are used to using this site and know how to navigate it. The online activity poses problems such as asking students to multiply two binomials and type the answer. The program keeps track of how many questions are answered, elapsed time, and a score that gauges mastery of the topic. Students can have scrap paper and pencils to help figure out the problems.

Some students finish the textbook problems quickly and begin to work on the laptops. Ms. Parks circulates the room to check on the progress of students still working on the first ten problems. Most students continue to finish their work and begin working on the laptops. A few students are still working, act disruptively, or raise their hands to ask questions because their answers do not match what is in the textbook. This gives Ms. Parks a chance to work one-on-one with the students who are struggling most with the textbook problems, and to keep a closer eye on the students who are having trouble working productively until math time is over. When the bell rings, all but three students have finished their assignment and were able to work on the laptops.

Reflection Questions

First consider Ms. Parks's use of technology in this lesson. Based on her perception of students' needs and preferences, she selected a computer activity that aligned with the content of the lesson, and also used her computer and projector to display the problems on the board. She and students solved the problems together.

- Would you consider this a technology-rich lesson? Why or why not?

- What was the purpose of Ms. Parks's technology use in this lesson?

- How did Ms. Parks's integration of technology advance the teaching and learning of math in this lesson?

- What were she and/or the students able to do with technology that was different from or better than what could have been done without technology?

Next, consider the math teaching practices in Ms. Parks's lesson.

- What were her goals for this math lesson?

- How did she address students' individual needs in this lesson?

- Would you describe this lesson as more teacher-centered or more student-centered? Why?

- To what extent did students have equitable access to learn and demonstrate their understanding in this lesson?

- Overall, what strengths do you see in this lesson? What opportunities do you notice?

Mr. Chavez's eighth-grade algebra class is also learning about multiplying binomials. As you read about Mr. Chavez's lesson, consider how he integrates technology in the lesson and his mathematical teaching practices.

 ## CASE 2.2

Mr. Chavez's Grade 8 Algebra Lesson

OBJECTIVES
- Use algebra tiles to accurately model multiplying binomials.
- Connect procedures for multiplying binomials with algebra tile models.

Mr. Chavez launches the lesson by asking students to model $3(x+2)$ with algebra tiles, then write the product. Students work individually at their seats to model this multiplication with a virtual algebra tile manipulative on their laptops, recording their solution on paper. As students work, Mr. Chavez circulates throughout the room, monitoring students' work, addressing questions, and requesting that students with inaccurate models or expressions compare and discuss their work with a neighboring student (specifically referring them to peers who he has observed to have accurate models and expressions).

Mr. Chavez then directs the students aloud: "Model $(x+1)(x+2)$ with algebra tiles. Then write an equation to express the product on paper or on the screen." Students work in pairs using virtual manipulatives and a product math background to solve the problem. While students are working, Mr. Chavez observes their work and addresses questions and misconceptions. He expects to see some students struggle with setting up the problem and multiplying both terms of the binomials. To these students, he asks questions such as: "What are the two factors that you are multiplying? Have you multiplied all of the terms? Can you combine any of the terms?" He makes note of students' work and strategies so he can call on students during whole-group discussion.

After all student pairs have solved the problem, Mr. Chavez initiates a whole-group discussion by inviting student A to show and explain how she began the problem.

As students share their algebra tile images and explain their reasoning, Mr. Chavez develops a written record of their work on the board. The written record scaffolds toward the procedure for multiplying binomials. Table 2.1 summarizes student explanations and images alongside Mr. Chavez's written record and questions/prompts.

TABLE 2.1 Student Explanations and Mr. Chavez's Record and Prompts

Student Explanation	Student Algebra Tile Images	Mr. Chavez's Written Record	Mr. Chavez's Questions and Prompts
Arya: So I put x+1 on the top and x+2 on the side	Representing (x+1)(x+2) with algebra tiles	(x+1)(x+2)	Do we all agree that Arya's picture shows (x+1)(x+2)? [Class agrees.] Ok, what next? Brendan?
Brendan: I just started by filling in the top row.	Multiplying x(x+1) with algebra tiles	(x+1)(x+2)	So, what does that mean? Mathematically, what are you doing when you fill in the top row? Catalina, how would you describe that?
Catalina: Well, you're multiplying the x on the side by the x+1 on the top. **Catalina:** An x2 and an x.	Show multiplication of x(x+1) $x^2 + x$ Connecting x(x+1) with x2 + x	$(x+1)(x+2) =$ $x2 + x$	Yes, could everyone hear that? You're multiplying the x from the x+2 on the side by the x+1 on the top. What do you get when you do that multiplication? One x2 and one x. Davon, can you show us what to do next?

Continued

Student Explanation	Student Algebra Tile Images	Mr. Chavez's Written Record	Mr. Chavez's Questions and Prompts
Davon: You multiplied the x on the side, so now you have to multiply the two ones on the side. You just fill in the rest.	Representing 2(x+1) Circling product of 2(x+1)	(x+1)(x+2) = x2 + x	Can you circle the part of the picture where you multiplied the two ones? Ok, Ella, can you add to what Davon just explained?
Ella: Yeah, um, Davon multiplied the two by the x+1 and now there's two x's and two ones. **Ella:** That's the 2x and the two because it's two times x+1..	Multiplying 2(x+1) Showing product of 2(x+1)	(x+1)(x+2) = x2 + x + 2x + 2	Ok, can you see that in what I just wrote? Where? Thumbs up if you understand what Davon and Ella just explained. I see a couple of folks don't look convinced. Farouk, what question do you have?

Continued

Student Explanation	Student Algebra Tile Images	Mr. Chavez's Written Record	Mr. Chavez's Questions and Prompts
Farouk: I get the filling in the blocks part, but how do we know to add all of that together like what you wrote? **Farouk:** (nods) **Farouk:** There's only one of the x2 pieces, and there's 1-2-3 x's and then two ones. **Farouk:** Yeah, ok. I see it now. x2+3x+2	Product of (x+1)(x+2) in algebra tiles Circling product of (x+1)(x+2)	$(x+1)(x+2) =$ $x2 + x + 2x + 2$ $(x+1)(x+2) = x2 + x + 2x + 2$ $x2 + 3x + 2$	Interesting question! Would you agree that the blocks we filled in are the result when we multiply (x+1)(x+2)? So all of this is the product. Let's think back to what we learned about combining like terms. Which ones can be combined? Exactly. If all of that is the product of (x+1)(x+2), then how do we express that symbolically? Who has something different? Gabriela?
Gabriela: My picture is the same, but I wrote 1x2. But I think that doesn't matter.	Writing product as an equation	$(x+1)(x+2) = x2 + x + 2x + 2$ $x2 + 3x + 2$ $1x2 = x2$	Yes, so 1x2 is equivalent to x2, you can write that either way. Most of the time we don't write the one though.
Hunter: When you multiply the x and the x, you get x2 in the equation. Then you multiply the x and the one which is x. Multiply the two by the x and you get 2 x's so you have three x's altogether now which is where the 3x comes from. And when you multiply 2 x 1, that's where the two comes from.	Connecting algebra tiles with equation	$(x+1)(x+2) = x2 + x + 2x + 2$ $x2 + 3x + 2$	Hunter, can you walk us through one more time how the algebra tiles match the equation?

Following the whole group discussion, Mr. Chavez projects three more problems. Students work individually to model these problems with algebra tiles, and record steps in multiplying the binomials symbolically.

$$(x+3)(x+5)= \underline{\quad} \qquad (2x+3)(x+4) = \underline{\quad} \qquad (x+6)(3x+4) = \underline{\quad}$$

While students are working, Mr. Chavez circulates and using a stop-motion app on his tablet, takes photos of steps in students' written work. He also asks students to take screenshots of their work with virtual manipulatives and send them to him. Within the app, he puts these images together to quickly create a short stop-motion video that shows algebra tiles and corresponding procedures for multiplying binomials.

As students finish the three problems, Mr. Chavez asks them to go to the IXL website and work on Multiply Two Polynomials using the algebra tiles topic.

To close the lesson, Mr. Chavez shows students the stop-motion video he created from the photos of students' work. He asks them to explain what the video shows, and relates this to the distributive property. Student explanations serve as a summary of what they learned in the lesson, namely to use algebra tiles to model multiplying binomials and connecting algebra tiles to the procedures for multiplying binomials (distributive property). He plans to launch tomorrow's lesson with a similar stop-motion video, and then challenge students to create their own videos to demonstrate the connections between Algebra tile representations and the procedures for multiplying binomials using the distributive property.

Reflection Questions

Now, let's consider Mr. Chavez's use of technology in this lesson. As you reflect and discuss, consider what happened in Mr. Chavez's lesson and how it compares with Ms. Parks's class.

- Would you consider this a technology-rich lesson? Why or why not?

- What was the purpose of Mr. Chavez's technology use in this lesson?

- How did Mr. Chavez's integration of technology advance the teaching and learning of math in this lesson?

- What were he and/or the students able to do with technology that was different from or better than what could have been done without technology?

Next, consider the mathematical teaching practices in Mr. Chavez's lesson and how they compare with the practices in the first scenario.

- What were Mr. Chavez's goals for this math lesson?

- How did he address students' individual needs in this lesson?

- Would you describe this lesson as more teacher-centered or more student-centered? Why?

- To what extent did students have equitable access to learn and demonstrate their understanding in this lesson?

- Overall, what strengths do you see in this lesson? What opportunities do you notice?

● ● ● ●

What Does the Research Say?

Following are research findings regarding technology as a motivator for student learning of math:

- Technology may well serve as an external motivator for some students, but that does not necessarily mean students will learn more effectively with technology. Studies of technology as a student motivator have found mixed, or weak, associations between technology use for learning mathematics and motivation for learning math.

- The positive effects of technology on motivation for learning math have often been intertwined with features of constructivist teaching practices such as exploratory and collaborative learning. This further supports our contention that technology use must be considered in conjunction with research-based math teaching practices.

- External motivators can make classroom experiences more "fun" for students, but more fun does not necessarily mean more effective. The use of tools and contexts to motivate mathematical learning must be purposefully connected to mathematical concepts in ways that engage students in learning more deeply. A focus on "fun" tools can, in some cases, be little more than a diversion from mathematical concepts.

The following math teaching practices support student learning:

- "To use mathematics effectively, students must be able to do much more than carry out mathematical procedures" (Martin, 2009, p. 165). Research tells us that when procedures are connected with, and built upon, a strong foundation of concepts, students will be better equipped to accurately apply procedures in new contexts. In fact, *Build Procedural Fluency from Conceptual Understanding* is identified by the National Council of Teachers of Mathematics as one of eight effective mathematics teaching practices (NCTM, 2014).

- Learning math extends far beyond getting the right answer; it involves a complex network of knowledge, skills, abilities, and beliefs. Mathematical proficiency, as defined by the National Research Council, is composed of five interwoven and interdependent strands: conceptual understanding, procedural fluency, strategic competence, adaptive reasoning, and productive disposition. Any teaching approach that focuses exclusively on procedural fluency does not address the breadth of what it means to become mathematically proficient.

- Procedural and computational fluency is related to students' number sense and understanding of mathematical structure. In introductory algebra, students may draw upon their conceptual understanding of whole number properties and operations, and apply those concepts as they learn to use the distributive property for multiplying new classes of problems such as binomials. This means it is important to give students opportunities to connect procedures with these concepts.

- Although a variety of "gimmicks" are often used to encourage and motivate students to learn mathematical facts and develop procedural fluency, rushing toward fluency can have an opposite effect. Mathematical understanding takes time, and too early of an emphasis on fluency can result in math anxiety and a loss of interest in the subject. Thus, technology use that rushes fluency before students have a solid conceptual foundation may have the opposite of the motivational effect you may intend.

Reflecting on Technology in Math Teaching

As you read the cases of Ms. Parks's and Mr. Chavez's eighth-grade classrooms, you should have noticed significant differences in how the math was taught and how technology was used to support math teaching. In Ms. Parks's class, she aligned her technology use toward a behavioral goal of using laptops to motivate students to complete the lesson. Her content goal was learning to multiply binomials algorithmically, using the FOIL method. Mr. Chavez aligned his technology use with a goal to connect among multiple representations of multiplying binomials (algebra tile models, equations, and verbal explanations). Although he did not express a behavioral goal for the use of technology, we can see that it was used as a tool to facilitate participation and mathematical discourse throughout the lesson. In both cases, we see evidence of alignment between goals and use of technology for teaching and learning math. However, although well-intentioned, Ms. Parks's goals do not necessarily align with what research tells us about teaching and learning math and about using technology for motivation. This helps to illustrate that aligning technology use with teaching, learning, and content is important, but may not be sufficient if it does not promote effective teaching and learning of rich math. Table 2.2 compares the use of technology in the two cases.

TABLE 2.2 Use of Technology in the Cases of Ms. Parks and Mr. Chavez

	The Case of Ms. Parks	**The Case of Mr. Chavez**
What technology is used?	Multiply binomials practice on IXL via laptops.	Virtual algebra tiles, screen-share on a projected device, stop-motion video, multiply binomials with algebra tiles practice on IXL via laptops.
What math is emphasized?	Carry out and practice algorithms for multiplying binomials.	Connect a visual model of binomial multiplication with the steps of an algorithmic approach using the distributive property.
How is the lesson launched?	Ms. Parks announces independent practice on laptops as a behavioral motivator at the beginning of the lesson, and then asks students to solve binomial multiplication problems and compare their solutions with a peer.	Mr. Chavez asks students to model a multiplication problem involving a monomial and binomial using algebra tiles, write a corresponding equation, and discuss with a peer, as needed.
Who is doing the math in this lesson?	Ms. Parks demonstrates the procedure as students follow along and practice the procedures.	Students use familiar algebra tiles to model binomial multiplication and share their thinking with the rest of the class to build shared understanding.
When and how is technology used in the lesson?	Students can practice the topic independently on laptops at the end of the lesson.	Students use virtual manipulatives to model multiplication and present their thinking to the class using projected screen-sharing software. Mr. Chavez displays a stop-motion video at the end of the lesson. Students can practice the topic independently on laptops at the end of the lesson.

A helpful lens for considering Ms. Parks's and Mr. Chavez's technology use in these lessons might be to ask: *"How does the use of technology in this lesson advance students' opportunities to learn meaningful math?"* If the math lesson does not offer opportunities to learn meaningful math in the first place, then it is unrealistic to expect that technology could transform student learning experiences in ways that align with what we know from research.

It is also important to consider the role technology plays in providing equitable access to learning math. In the case of Ms. Parks, students who met the objective first had first access to technology, while those who struggled the most were last to use the computers. Furthermore, the computer application seemed to be part of a rush to computational fluency that does not align with what research tells us about learning math. If we view technology as a reward for students who are already successful in math, we diminish the opportunity for technology to serve as a tool for supporting learning for those who may need it most. On the other hand, students in Mr. Chavez's classroom each used technology early in the lesson to model binomial multiplication and connect between a visual model and an algorithm. Every student had an opportunity to use technology as a tool for connecting among multiple representations, not as an add-on, but as a main part of the learning experience. The class discussion then engaged many students in sharing and explaining their representations and connections. Although students could have also used physical manipulatives for much of this activity, the use of virtual manipulatives facilitated sharing students' representations. (Once norms and expectations for devices are well-established in the classroom, virtual manipulatives may require less materials management than physical versions.)

Recommendations for Practice

At the beginning of this chapter, we posed the following question: *Instead of using technology as a gimmick to "trick" students into learning math, what if technology were to be used as an instructional tool to enhance the learning of rich mathematical concepts?*

Vignettes from Ms. Parks's and Mr. Chavez's classrooms offer an example of what this shift might look like in a secondary classroom. But what can you do to effectively motivate rich mathematical learning with technology in your classroom? Here are three suggestions with accompanying elaboration and examples.

1. Establish mathematical learning goals that emphasize conceptual understanding and developing fluency from understanding.

Then, select technologies that align with those goals and are accessible to students. Implement apps and games that emphasize skill and drill only after students have developed understanding. Drill should increase speed and automaticity, but does little to support students who don't understand the math in the first place.

For example, when students are learning to add and subtract integers, a goal might be to efficiently and accurately add and subtract positive and negative integers. A quick online search of "add integers" yields many possible games that quiz students' algorithmic fluency in potentially engaging contexts, but without any representational or conceptual connections. Although it's easy to find many games that align with the previously stated goal, neither the games nor the goal provide students with an opportunity to develop conceptual understanding of operations with integers.

Although it is important that students are eventually able to compute efficiently and accurately, students should first experience multiple opportunities to develop understanding of integers and notice patterns with operations involving positive and negative numbers. Consider an earlier goal such as: "Determine when the sum of two integers will be positive or negative." In this case, one might seek out games that feature visual models (e.g., funbrain.com's Line Jumper or xpmath.com's Roll Back Number Line). Technology aligned with this goal might also include virtual manipulatives and resources such as Math Learning Center's interactive Number Line app or Braining Camp's two-color chips, which provide students opportunities to explore these relationships. Technology choices that are aligned with strong learning goals provide opportunities for students to develop conceptual understanding, whereas computational fluency games may only assess what students already know.

2. Use technology to support good teaching, rather than as an add-on to the lesson.

Planning lessons that integrate appropriate technology in the teaching of math are more impactful and equitable than including technology only if there's time, or for students who finish early.

Technology that is made available "only if there's time" is not truly integrated into the lesson, and is likely to go unused by many students. Time may be teachers' most precious resource, and few teachers have time to spare during the school day. Why then plan for technology use that is unlikely to occur? The time that you spend bookmarking sites, distributing devices, or managing resources for "add-on" technology use could be better spent engaging all students in meaningful learning opportunities. Furthermore, when technology is positioned as a privilege for some students, its true value as a teaching and learning resource is undermined. (Imagine if textbooks or whiteboards were available only to students who met behavioral goals or finished their work early.) A more powerful and equitable use of technology resources is in the planning and enactment of the actual math lesson. If the selected technology assesses students' mathematical skills, why not incorporate it in lieu of an exit ticket or quiz during the lesson? Rather than adding a chance to explore with an applet or virtual manipulative at the end of the lesson, why not build in those opportunities as part of your teaching while students are learning new concepts? Instead of using a video or webpage to show early finishers how the math in your lesson might apply in "real life," why not capture all students' interest by launching the lesson with that same video or resource?

3. Leverage the novelty of technology to illuminate, not hide, the math that students are learning.

Elaborate graphics, sound effects, and gaming contexts may be appealing, but ask yourself: "Is this helping students to engage and learn, or is it tricking them into something they may not recognize as math later on?"

In 1978, an Apple II personal computer promotional brochure featured the phrase: "Simplicity is the ultimate sophistication," a precursor to the minimalist aesthetic that would become synonymous with the tech giant. This "less is more" idea can also be a useful consideration for integrating technology in to your classroom. Although funny cartoon characters and silly noises might be appealing features of a website or app, do they help students learn math? Not unless they are paired mathematically rich experiences that align with how students learn. No matter the bells and whistles, using technology for drilling facts is typically little more than a high-tech replacement for flash cards. If this approach helps capture the attention of students who otherwise would hesitate to engage in practice, it may be useful. But practicing procedures is but a small component of learning math. On the other hand, tools such as screencasting (e.g., Screencastomatic, Explain Everything, Educreations, ShowMe) provide a blank slate where users can write, capture images, and record audio to reveal thinking. Though these tools offer less novelty at first glance, they enable teachers and students to communicate representations, strategies, and thinking in ways that can be transformative in a math classroom. In general, select technology resources not for how they look, but for what they can do in your math teaching!

Connecting Cases with Standards

In this chapter, the case of Mr. Chavez illustrates many opportunities for effective math teaching with technology. Here, we present how the lesson aligns with Common Core State Standards for Mathematics in terms of both content and practices. We also offer alignment with ISTE Standards for Students and for Educators. It may be useful for you to discuss and consider with colleagues how the case aligns with math standards in your state or district, as well as ISTE Standards for Administrators and for Coaches.

Math Content Standard

CCSS.MATH. CONTENT.HSA.APR.A.1 Understand that polynomials form a system analogous to the integers, namely, they are closed under the operations of addition, subtraction, and multiplication; add, subtract, and multiply polynomials.

Mathematical Practice Standards

- Make sense of problems and persevere in solving them

- Reason abstractly and quantitatively

- Construct viable arguments and critique the reasoning of others

- Use appropriate tools strategically

- Attend to precision

- Look for and make use of structure

ISTE Standards for Educators

5b. Design authentic learning activities that align with content area standards and use digital tools and resources to maximize active, deep learning.

6c. Create learning opportunities that challenge students to use a design process and computational thinking to innovate and solve problems.

7a. Provide alternative ways for students to demonstrate competency and reflect on their learning using technology.

ISTE Standards for Students

5c. Students break problems into component parts, extract key information, and develop descriptive models to understand complex systems or facilitate problem-solving.

6c. Students communicate complex ideas clearly and effectively by creating or using a variety of digital objects such as visualizations, models or simulations.

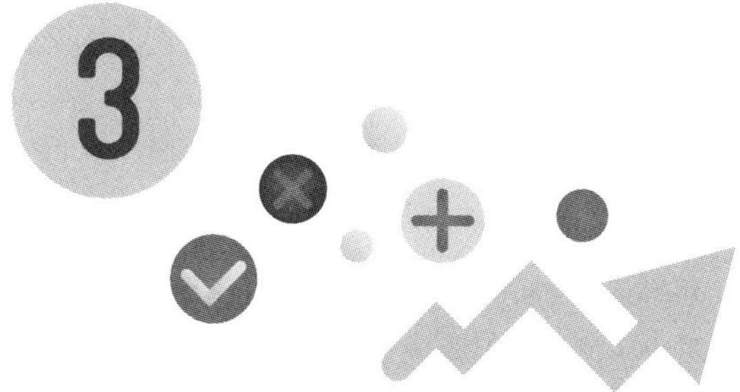

MOVING FROM INDIVIDUALIZED INSTRUCTION TO TECHNOLOGY FOR COLLABORATIVE LEARNING

Instead of using screens to enable disconnected, individualized learning, what if we leveraged technology to facilitate mathematical discourse and collaboration?

THIS CHAPTER INCLUDES two cases that illustrate teaching fraction equivalence with technology tools in an Algebra I class. As you read each of the following cases, consider how and what math is being taught, how technology is being used, and how the two connect. After reading and reflecting on the two cases, compare your insights and connections with what research has to say about two big ideas illustrated in the cases: *Technology as a Collaborative Tool* and *Teaching Practices that Support Mathematical Learning.* You might also take a moment to examine how each of the lessons aligns with standards for math content, mathematical practices; and ISTE Standards for students, educators, and coaches. Standards alignment is offered at the end of the chapter for your reference.

Technology as a Collaborative Tool

Technology can be used to connect, collaborate, and communicate among students and teachers. Indeed, collaboration and communication are consistently listed among digital age skills that educators wish to develop among students. Simultaneously, teachers and administrators face calls for more personalized learning, ranging from the ISTE Standard for Educators, *5a. Use technology to create, adapt, and personalize learning experiences that foster independent learning and accommodate learner differences and needs,* to individualized learning programs marketed by tech companies. For teachers looking to address all of these goals, there may be perceived tension between using technology to collaborate and communicate and using technology to personalize learning. In a math classroom, how can students communicate and collaborate if each student is working individually at their own pace? How can a teacher encourage mathematical discourse if each student is at a different place in a unit facilitated by a personalized learning program? Reconciling these tensions is an essential component of utilizing technology in a way that supports students' individual needs.

Teaching Practices that Support Math Learning

Well-known learning theorist Lev Vygotsky wrote: "What a child can do in cooperation today, [s/]he can do alone tomorrow." Teaching that encourages students to engage in mathematical discussions not only supports cooperation and collaboration, but also provides them with opportunities to articulate and refine their reasoning through language and multimodal forms of communication. Classrooms rich in mathematical discourse support students' mathematical learning by allowing them to collaboratively develop shared understanding. By honoring and discussing students' diverse contributions and ways of thinking, teachers can support learner differences and needs. Mathematical discourse communities can differentiate for students' individual needs by meeting students where they are in their learning, and leveraging partner, small-group, and whole-group interactions to build upon the math that students know and can do. A focus on collaboration and communication in the classroom can also emphasize reasoning and concepts, rather than narrowly defining math in terms of right or wrong answers. Rather than isolating students to learn math at individual screens, technology can support classroom discourse communities that engage students in collaboration and mathematical communication.

In the following case, Ms. King's Algebra I class is learning about comparing linear functions using tables, graphs, equations, and verbal descriptions. Consider how she integrates technology into the lesson and her math teaching practices. How does she use technology to encourage communication and collaboration? To what extent does technology and instruction support personalized learning experiences that accommodate learner differences?

 CASE 3.1

Ms. King's Algebra I Comparing Linear Functions Lesson

OBJECTIVES

* Compare linear functions represented graphically, in tables, as equations, or by verbal descriptions.

Ms. King's classroom has 1:1 computers. Her school has recently begun encouraging more personalized learning experiences using classroom technology and free online open educational resources. The goal of this initiative is to improve students' performance on state assessments through more individualized learning experiences using technology. This aligns with Ms. King's goals of designing instruction that meets her students' diverse needs and strengths.

To implement personalized learning in her classroom, Ms. King and her students use Khan Academy. Through their free, online resources, she is able to set up her class; assign lessons, videos, exercises, and quizzes; and view students' progress and scores. She appreciates that the online resources save time that she would spend on grading, but realizes that she spends a similar amount of time setting up and monitoring the online class and data.

Since implementing personalized learning in her classroom, one of the challenges Ms. King has faced is pacing. There is tension between meeting the district's scope-and-sequence with their adopted curriculum while also allowing students to learn at their own pace in the online environment. She addresses this by starting each unit with lessons from the textbook, then giving students several days to work at their own pace to complete online lessons that are comparable to what is in her curriculum materials. A few days before the end of each unit, Ms. King will review and reteach using lessons from the textbook, and then her students will take the district's unit assessments.

Lately, Ms. King's class has been learning about linear functions and comparing across repre-sentations. Together as a whole group, Ms. King shows students the first Khan Academy video in the Interpreting Linear Functions and Equations lesson, and answers student questions. After watching the video together, students may rewatch the video, proceed to new videos in the lesson, complete the exercises, or proceed to the next lesson about comparing linear functions. Students work online at their own pace until they have taken the online quiz for these two lessons. The videos, practice exercises, and quiz include finding equivalent fractions using numerals, bar models, area models of various shapes, and number lines. Exercises are numerical or selected-response.

Some students finish both lessons and the quiz in one day. For these students, Ms. King assigns enrichment work from the textbook or lets them work on homework. Other students are still struggling to earn a passing quiz score at the end of the second day. As students work online during class, Ms. King spends some of her time assisting those students. Other times, she monitors students as they work individually, making sure they are on-task. When she is not working with individual students or monitoring the classroom, she often checks student progress through the data available to her online.

Ms. King is happy to be contributing to the vision of more personalized learning in her school, but has some mixed feelings about how it is going. She hasn't noticed a major difference in unit test scores as compared to her colleagues who aren't using personalized learning in their classrooms, but she has data to show that her students are progressing through the lessons. She has noticed that the classroom is generally quieter during math now, but there is less opportunity for the partner and group work in math that she believes is important for learning math. Some students have had a more difficult time staying on task lately. Ms. King is excited about how she and her students are using technology for learning math, but continues to reflect on the right balance between personalized learning, her school's math curriculum, and her teaching philosophy in order to best meet her students' diverse needs.

Reflection Questions

Consider Ms. King's use of technology in this lesson. Based on her perception of students' needs and district preferences, she selected a technology that aligned with the math content she needed to teach.

- Would you consider this a technology-rich lesson? Why or why not?

- What was the purpose of Ms. King's technology use in this lesson?

- How did Ms. King's integration of technology advance the teaching and learning in this math lesson?

- What were she and/or the students able to do with technology that was different from or better than what could have been done without technology?

- Might the use of technology in this lesson hinder students' math learning in any way? Why or why not?

Next, consider the math teaching practices in Ms. King's lesson.

- What were Ms. King's goals for this math lesson?

- How did she address students' individual needs in this lesson?

- Would you describe this lesson as more teacher-centered or more student-centered? Why?

- To what extent did students have equitable access to learn and demonstrate their understanding in this lesson?

- Overall, what strengths do you see in this lesson? What opportunities do you notice?

Mr. Lennon's Algebra I class is also learning about comparing linear functions. As you read about Mr. Lennon's lesson, consider how he integrates technology into the lesson and his mathematical teaching practices. How does he use technology to encourage communication and collaboration? To what extent does technology and instruction support personalized learning experiences that accommodate learner differences?

 ## CASE 3.2

Mr. Lennon's Algebra I Comparing Linear Functions Lesson

OBJECTIVES
- Compare linear functions represented graphically, in tables, as equations, or by verbal descriptions.

Mr. Lennon knows that some students continue to struggle with recognizing linear functions across multiple representations. He is using today as an extra lesson to supplement the lessons in his district-adopted curriculum materials. Before engaging students in comparing properties of functions, he has designed an online card sort, using Desmos, that gives them an opportunity to think and reason about functions presented in graphs, tables, equations, and contextual situations. He wants students to work together and discuss their reasoning, so he has assigned partners for whom he knows can work productively.

At the beginning of the lesson, Mr. Lennon pairs students, and asks one student from each pair to get a laptop from a cart in the back of the room. While students are getting their computers, he projects the student.desmos.com web address and class codes so that all students can log on promptly. He tells students that their task is to sort the linear function cards into four categories, and that they will need to discuss with their partners to decide on the categories. The card sort activity (shown in Figure 3.1) includes a total of 16 cards that could be sorted in a variety of ways depending on how students reason about them.

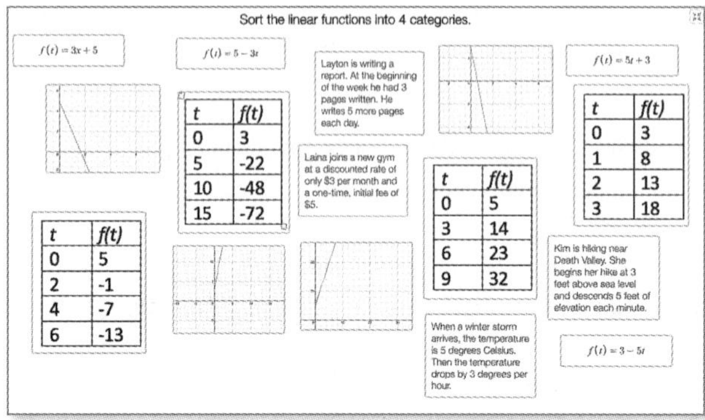

Figure 3.1 Linear function card sort.

As students work on the online card sort, Mr. Lennon views their results on the teacher.desmos.com dashboard. He accurately anticipates that some students will sort the cards by representation type, some will try to match a different type of representation for each of the four functions but make errors in matching some of the representations, and some students will successfully match the representation types for each of the four functions described. He invites three student pairs to explain their sort and categories to the whole group.

The first pair, Colin and Sonny, sorted by representation type. He displays their work on the board (see Figure 3.2) and asks them to explain their reasoning.

Sonny explains, "We saw four different kinds of problems, so we made a category for the functions that looked like this [points at symbolic equations], the tables of points, the graphs, and the word problems."

Mr. Lennon asks if the class agrees that those four categories make sense and that their grouping in those categories is accurate. No one indicates disagreement. "Let's look at another idea that Amaris and Maggie had for the categories." He displays their work, shown in Figure 3.3.

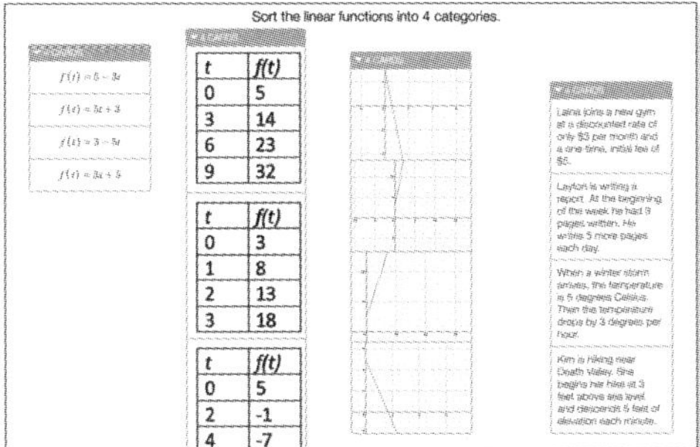

Figure 3.2 Colin and Sonny's card sort.

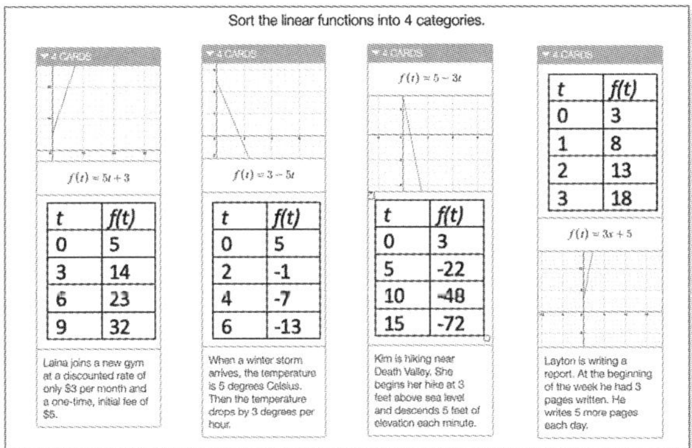

Figure 3.3 Amaris and Maggie's card sort.

"We sort of thought we were supposed to group them so that each category had one of each kind of function in it, and so they matched," says Maggie.

Mr. Lennon reiterates, "Maggie and Amaris decided that each of their categories would have the same function, but represented in four different ways: graph, equation, table, and a contextual situation." He chose Amaris and Maggie to present, knowing their matches weren't accurate. Mr. Lennon suspects they are confusing slope and y-intercept, and that other students may be making the same errors, so he invites them to further explain their choices within each category.

Amaris tells the class, "The first one we could see was going up on the graph, so we knew that the numbers needed to be positive in the equation, and we could see that the numbers were going up in the table. It took us a while to figure out which word problem would fit, but because the fee was $5, we decided that one made the most sense."

"How did you decide that f(t)=5t+3 matched instead of f(t)=3t+5. You said that the numbers needed to be positive in the equation, but everything is positive in both of those equations. Can you tell us more about that?" asks Mr. Lennon.

"Because it starts at five, we picked the equation that starts with five," Amaris replies. A few students raise their hand. Mr. Lennon asks Meg to add to what Amaris said.

"I think even though the equation starts with five, because it's 5t, that means it goes up by five each time. Wouldn't that equation start at three? Because if we think of it like y=mx+b equations, then in f(t)=5t+3, five would be the slope, and three would be the intercept, which is like the starting point," adds Meg.

Mr. Lennon senses that Amaris and Maggie are unsure, so he gives the class a couple minutes of think-time to discuss in pairs and small groups. He suggests that they try some of the ordered pairs from the table to help them figure out which equation is accurate.

Amaris and Maggie come to agree with Meg's accurate assertion. "We see what Meg means now. It makes more sense if we switch the equations [f(t)=5t+3 and f(t)=3t+5]. We tried using the numbers from the table, like you said, and the first one with Laina and the gym works if the equation is f(t)=3x+5, but you don't get the right numbers with f(t)=3t+5."

"Malia and Jordin have four categories that look a lot like what Amaris and Maggie have come up with. Let's take a look at theirs and see what we think about it." Mr. Lennon displays their work for the class to see (as shown in Figure 3.4). Students agree that their groupings make sense. He asks them to explain one of the categories with negative slope.

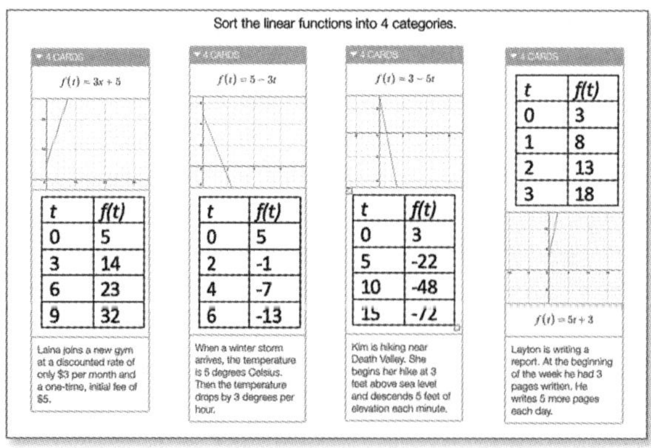

t	f(t)
0	5
3	14
6	23
9	32

t	f(t)
0	5
2	-1
4	-7
6	-13

t	f(t)
0	3
5	-22
10	-48
15	-72

t	f(t)
0	3
1	8
2	13
3	18

Figure 3.4 Malia and Jordin's card sort.

Jordin explains, "With the Death Valley one, we could see that the graph crossed the axis at three, and the line was going down pretty steep so we picked f(t)=3-5t as the equation. That one also matches with the table that shows zero and three, and then goes down. When we looked at the word problem part, it says she started at three feet above sea level so that would be positive three, and then it goes down five feet per minute. At first we thought maybe the table was wrong because it goes down by more than five, but then we realized that it was showing five minutes, not one minute, so it was ok."

After the whole-group discussion about different representations for linear functions, Mr. Lennon tells the class that they are going to use what they just discussed, and compare some of the properties of linear functions that are shown using different representations. He tells them to go to Khan Academy and find the Comparing Linear Functions lesson. Students are expected to continue working as partners to successfully complete the two sets of practice exercises and quiz. Mr. Lennon can monitor their progress though the Khan Academy teacher dashboard and provide one-on-one support, as needed. Some students successfully proceed straight to the practice exercises and quiz. Others view some of the videos to help them with the exercises. As Mr. Lennon circulates around the classroom to monitor and provide support, he reminds students of the videos and hints accompanying practice problems. He notices some are struggling to do the work in their head, so he encourages them to use the built-in calculator, or pencil and paper, to help them figure out the problems. Students who finish early can proceed to the next Khan lessons on Linear Models Word Problems.

When students are finished with the Khan Academy quiz, Mr. Lennon asks the class to go back to the Desmos tab from the beginning of class. He displays a question slide (the question is shown in Figure 3.5) that relates to the types of problems students just solved online. Still working with their partners on the laptops, students are asked to enter multiple-choice responses to the question about comparing three linear functions, each with a different type of representation. Mr. Lennon can see that most students answered the question correctly. He calls on one student to briefly explain his reasoning to the rest of the class.

Jesse explains, "For the first one, I plugged in three for t and got P=$33.50. For the second one, I just multiplied $5 times three days and added $10, so Kai has $25. For Trina, I figured that because three is halfway between two and four, then it would be $32, which is halfway between $28 and $36. Alex would have the most then."

Mr. Lennon goes to the next screen (the contents of which are shown in Figure 3.6), and asks students to select whether Alex, Kai, or Trina would be the first to earn $100. He encourages them to use scratch paper, and confer with their partner as they work on the problem.

Alex, Kai, and Trina are saving money to go to an amusement park. Who will have the most money saved on Day 3?

- o Alex is earning money by walking her uncle's dog. This function represents the amount of money, P, she earns per day, t:
  $P = 3.5t + 23$
- o Kai has $10 when he starts saving. He earns $5 per day helping his neighbor with her garden.
- o Trina earns money for doing chores each day. The table shows her savings, P, on a given day, t.

T	P
0	20
2	28
4	36
6	44

Figure 3.5 Who will have the most money on day three?

Alex, Kai, and Trina are saving money to go to an amusement park. Who will be the first to earn the $100 needed for admission, food, and spending money?

- o Alex is earning money by walking her uncle's dog. This function represents the amount of money, P, she earns per day, t:
  $P = 3.5t + 23$
- o Kai has $10 when he starts saving. He earns $5 per day helping his neighbor with her garden.
- o Trina earns money for doing chores each day. The table shows her savings, P, on a given day, t.

T	P
0	20
2	28
4	36
6	44

Figure 3.6 Who will earn $100 first?

Fewer students correctly respond to this problem. With class time running out, Mr. Lennon asks students to jot the problem down in their notebooks, work on it more as homework, and be ready to discuss the problem at the beginning of class tomorrow.

Reflection Questions

Consider Mr. Lennon's use of technology in this lesson. As you reflect and discuss with colleagues, consider what happened in Mr. Lennon's lesson and how it compares with Ms. King's class.

- Would you consider this a technology-rich lesson? Why or why not?

- What was the purpose of Mr. Lennon's technology use in this lesson?

- How did Mr. Lennon's integration of technology advance the teaching and learning in this math lesson?

- What were he and/or the students able to do with technology that was different from or better than what could have been done without technology?

- Might the use of technology in this lesson hinder students' math learning in any way? Why or why not?

Next, consider Mr. Lennon's math teaching practices in this lesson and how they compare with the practices in the first scenario.

- What were Mr. Lennon's goals for this math lesson?

- How did he address students' individual needs in this lesson?

- Would you describe this lesson as more teacher-centered or more student-centered? Why?

- To what extent did students have equitable access to learn and demonstrate their understanding in this lesson?

- Overall, what strengths do you see in this lesson? What opportunities do you notice?

● ● ● ●

What Does the Research Say?

The following research supports the use of technology as a collaborative tool:

- Technology allows for networking, communicating, and collaborating in increasingly sophisticated ways. In a digitally connected world, students from across the classroom, or across the world, can communicate and work collaboratively in real time. Decades of research has shown that student engagement in collaborative, connected learning environments can positively impact their motivation, conceptual understanding, and perseverance for solving challenging problems, and has been shown to be particularly impactful for struggling learners. Furthermore, studies involving collaborative interactions with technology have shown more equitable participation than what often occurs in classroom discussions absent of technology. (See, for instance, Beatty & Geiger, 2009; Goos, Galbraith, Renshaw, & Geiger, 2000; Hoadley, Hsi, & Berman, 1995; Hsi & Hoadley, 1997; Hurme & Jarvela, 2005; Riel, 1991; Roschelle et al., 2010; Scardamalia & Bereiter, 1993; Suthers, Toth, & Weiner, 1997; White, 2006)

- Use of technology as a collaborative tool aligns with prevailing learning theories in math education. Whereas technology-enabled personalized learning approaches overwhelmingly employ behaviorist approaches to teaching and learning math (Dishon, 2017), math education research has, for decades, emphasized and drawn upon constructivist and socio-cultural theories (Cobb, 1994) for supporting more equitable student learning through collaborative, inquiry-driven, and discourse-rich teaching approaches. Using technology as a collaborative tool aligns with theory and research in math education. Using technology to personalize learning with behaviorist approaches that do not afford collaboration and communication can disregard decades of research on teaching and learning math.

- When students spend a significant amount of class time engaged individually with technology, mathematical discussion in the classroom can decrease (Thomas, 2013). However, the opposite can be true when students engage in models of personalized learning that include opportunities to work collaboratively with peers. Technology can impact the nature of human interactions and the interactions among learners, teachers, mathematical knowledge, and learning contexts (Borba et al., 2016). Plainly stated, using technology as a collaborative tool while also promoting personalized learning goals is a complex endeavor for teachers of math.

Following are mathematical teaching practices that support student learning:

- In developing a framework of high-leverage, effective mathematics teaching practices, the National Council of Teachers of Mathematics (2014) highlights research-based principles of learning including, "Learners should have experiences that enable them to construct knowledge socially, through discourse, activity, and interaction related to meaningful problems" (p. 9). A body of research, conducted over decades, continues to emphasize the importance of discourse and social knowledge construction for learning mathematics.

- Mathematical discourse includes focused classroom discussion around mathematical ideas, as well as other forms of communication. Mathematical discourse enables students to develop understanding through constructing, sharing, critiquing, clarifying, and refining their own ideas and those of others. The multimodal nature of mathematical discourse opens possibilities for technology to support this important component of learning math.

- Researchers have identified a number of strategies to support and facilitate meaningful mathematical discourse in classrooms. The five practices for orchestrating classroom discussions (Smith & Stein, 2011) suggest that teachers in whole class contexts anticipate possible student thinking before a lesson, monitor students' mathematical work, select specific students to present their work in a particular sequence, and connect across student work to highlight the math they want students to learn. Math talk moves (Chapin, O'Connor, & Anderson, 2013) offer another strategy for engaging students in partner, small-group, and whole-group discussions about math.

- In contrast to teaching and learning through mathematical discourse in collaborative contexts, individualized instruction is an approach that typically draws from a behaviorist approach to learning. A classic case study in math education (Erlwanger, 1973) highlights a sixth grade student, Benny, who used an individualized curriculum in the 1970s, the goal of which was, "… 'to develop an educational program which is maximally adaptive to the requirements of the individual' Lindvall & Cox, 1970, p. 34)" (p. 88).. Although Benny performed well within the (non technological) program, researchers revealed a number of misunderstandings and error patterns in his mathematical conception of rules and answers. The role of discussion, or lack thereof, is described in the study, "There is never any reason for Benny to participate in a discussion with either his teachers or his peers about what he has learned and what his views are about mathematics. Nevertheless, Benny has his own views about mathematics—its rules and its answers" (Erlwanger, 1973, p. 52). As teachers grapple with incorporating technology-enabled personalized learning programs in modern classrooms, this seminal study offers a precautionary tale about individualized mathematics instruction and the need to balance discourse about concepts with practice of procedures.

Reflecting on Technology in Math Teaching

As you read the cases of Ms. King's and Mr. Lennon's Algebra I classrooms, you should have noticed significant differences in how the math was taught and how technology was used to support their math teaching. In Ms. King's class, she aligned her technology use toward a mathematical goal of comparing linear equations using various representations and a technology goal of more personalized learning to meet individual needs. Mr. Lennon aligned his technology use with the same content goal, but used technology to facilitate collaboration and discourse to meet and leverage individualized needs and assets. In both cases, we see evidence of alignment between goals and use of technology for teaching and learning math. Ms. King has embraced a technology goal for personalized learning, but acknowledges some concerns resulting from that approach. The way she is using technology for personalized learning does not necessarily align with what research tells us about the nature of learning math. This helps to illustrate that aligning technology use with content goals and technology-use initiatives is important, but tensions can arise when technology use conflicts with what research and theory tell us about teaching and learning math (with or without technology). Table 3.3 compares the cases of Ms. King and Mr. Lennon.

TABLE 3.3 Use of Technology in the Cases of Ms. King and Mr. Lennon

	The Case of Ms. King	The Case of Mr. Lennon
What technology is used?	1:1 laptops; online personalized lessons, videos, exercises, and quiz from Khan Academy.	Online card sort through Desmos; online videos, exercises, and quiz from Khan Academy; interactive slides through Desmos.
What math is emphasized?	Comparing linear functions using verbal descriptions, equations, tables, and graphs.	Identifying multiple representations of linear functions, and comparing features of linear functions.
How is the lesson launched?	Ms. King shows a demonstrative video at the beginning of the first class, and then students work independently to progress through two lessons and a quiz.	Mr. Lennon uses Desmos to engage students in a sort of linear functions represented as graphs, tables, equations, and contextual situations. He uses partner talk and class discussion to launch a discussion about linear function representations.
Who is doing the math in this lesson?	Students watch videos that explain comparing linear functions and then complete practice questions and quizzes individually.	Students work with a partner to sort linear function representations in a digital environment, complete Khan Academy online exercises, and compare features of linear functions on Desmos slides.
When and how is technology used in the lesson?	The lesson is almost completely conveyed through personalized learning technology.	Mr. Lennon uses technology to launch the lesson, facilitates student collaboration and discussion through an online card sort, assesses students as they work together, and facilitates discussion and assesses students' understanding at the end of the lesson.

A helpful lens for considering Ms. King's and Mr. Lennon's technology use in these lessons might be to ask: *"How does the use of technology in this lesson align with effective math teaching practices?"* Because the math lesson relies on technology-enabled pedagogy that runs counter to research and best practices for teaching and learning math, it is not surprising that Ms. King has mixed feelings about the outcomes of her approach.

It is also important to consider the role technology plays in providing equitable access to math learning. Ms. King was motivated, in part, to use technology-enabled personalized learning to meet individualized student needs. Students could work at their own pace to some extent (within the constraints of her scope and sequence), and the arrangement allowed her more one-on-one time to assist students who were struggling. However, she noticed that some of her students had more difficulty focusing during individual computer-based learning, suggesting that the approach did not work the same with all students. Although the methodology enabled some individualized pacing, all students ended up doing the same work in, more or less, the same way.

On the other hand, students in Mr. Lennon's classroom used technology collaboratively throughout the lesson. Students worked together to complete a sorting activity online, and then Mr. Lennon facilitated a classroom discussion based on their technology-enabled work. Even though some student contributions weren't completely correct, Mr. Lennon leveraged all student contributions to highlight important student thinking about linear function representations. To move from recognizing representations to comparing linear functions, he had students complete online practice exercises. In doing so, Mr. Lennon also let students choose which videos and online features they found useful for completing the exercises. Throughout the lesson, all students had an opportunity to use the same technologies in ways that supported collaboration and communication about equivalent fractions.

Recommendations for Practice

This chapter began with the question: *Instead of screens to enable disconnected, individualized learning, what if we leveraged technology to facilitate mathematical discourse and collaboration?* Vignettes from Ms. King's and Mr. Lennon's classrooms show contrasting visions of what these two ideas could look like in secondary classrooms. How can you leverage technology to facilitate mathematical discourse and collaboration? Here are three suggestions with accompanying elaboration and examples.

1. Make sure students have a chance to engage in mathematical discourse during every lesson.

Technology should support communication and collaboration, not replace it. Giving students an opportunity to communicate mathematically lets them know their ideas are worth sharing. A variety of technologies can support sharing. In this case, the teacher used Desmos to facilitate a card sort, and facilitated a math discussion around students' responses. The technology enabled him to easily view all student responses, and to select, sequence, and display student work for discussion. Other tools such as Pear Deck and Near Pod can also elicit student work, but the mathematical capabilities in Desmos make it an attractive option for secondary math teachers. A variety of technologies allow the teacher to display student contributions for class discussion.

You could also use technology to facilitate mathematical communication in nonverbal formats. Through tools such as Google Classroom, Edmodo, or classroom blogs, students can share pictures or written accounts of their mathematical reasoning. Asking students to examine, discuss, or comment on one another's contributions supports the Common Core mathematical practice, MP3. *Construct viable arguments and critique the reasoning of others.*

2. Technology can, and should, support effective teaching practices, but technology won't replace the teacher!

Fill in the blank: "_________ today not only rivals formal education, but better yet, it increasingly is being used to supplement the work of the teacher." Did you guess internet? Computers? Maybe even television? This is the opening sentence of an article entitled, "Radio in the Classroom" from 1942! The tension between technology and teacher in the classroom is nearly a century old, but technology has yet to replace teachers.

Technology can change the role of teachers and students. In this chapter, two vignettes showed how Khan Academy could be used in different ways to support different teacher and student roles. The same could be said of tools such as IXL or DreamBox Learning. Technologies that offer personalized experiences for learners can supplement good classroom instruction without supplanting the teacher. Regardless of what technology a teacher chooses to use, it is important to evaluate how it fits with your teaching practices and reflect on classroom roles. If your teaching is guided by constructivist or sociocultural learning theories, consider how your technology use aligns with your priorities. If students are staring at isolated screens in a direct transmission model of learning math, reconsider what and how they are expected to learn math.

3. Use technology to facilitate a variety of collaboration structures.

In some contexts, sharing technology is necessary due to limited device availability. In other situations, students have access to 1:1 devices. Whether they share devices or have their own, technology can be used in ways that promote collaboration. Tools such as connected whiteboard apps or G Suite collaborative apps (Docs, Sheets, Slides) enable real-time collaboration on written or visual projects. In a secondary math classroom, students can use digital collaborative spaces to share their thinking in writing or create presentations of their work to share with the class.

Students can also collaborate with partners on shared devices. Working together to solve a card sort in Desmos or to represent a mathematical problem using a virtual manipulative requires both cooperation and communication. You can use videos to pose interesting problems to groups of students who then work collaboratively to find solutions. 3-act tasks from gfletchy.com or Dan Meyer (blog.mrmeyer.com) leverage technology to pose questions that do not require individual devices, but invite collaboration and mathematical discussion. Using technology (interactive whiteboard, projector, screencasts) to select and display student work with interesting tasks can also encourage collaboration and mathematical discussion.

Connecting Cases with Standards

In this chapter, the cases of Ms. King and Mr. Lennon demonstrate ways that technology can be used to teach an Algebra I lesson on comparing linear functions. Following, you will find alignment with Common Core State Standards for Mathematics, as well as ISTE Standards for Students and for Educators. It may be useful to discuss and consider with colleagues how the case aligns with math standards in your state or district, as well as ISTE Standards for Administrators and for Coaches.

Math Content Standard

CCSS.MATH.CONTENT.8.FA.2/CCSS.MATH.CONTENT.IF.C9. Compare properties of two functions each represented in a different way (algebraically, graphically, numerically in tables, or by verbal descriptions).

Mathematical Practice Standards

- Make sense of problems and persevere in solving them

- Reason abstractly and quantitatively

- Construct viable arguments and critique the reasoning of others

- Attend to precision

ISTE Standards for Educators

5a. Use technology to create, adapt and personalize learning experiences that foster independent learning and accommodate learner differences and needs.

5b. Design authentic learning activities that align with content area standards and use digital tools and resources to maximize active, deep learning.

6a. Foster a culture where students take ownership of their learning goals and outcomes in both independent and group settings.

6b. Manage the use of technology and student learning strategies in digital platforms, virtual environments, hands-on makerspaces or in the field.

7b. Use technology to design and implement a variety of formative and summative assessments that accommodate learner needs, provide timely feedback to students and inform instruction.

7c. Use assessment data to guide progress and communicate with students, parents and education stakeholders to build student self-direction.

ISTE Standards for Students

1c. Students use technology to seek feedback that informs and improves their practice and to demonstrate their learning in a variety of ways.

4d. Students exhibit a tolerance for ambiguity, perseverance and the capacity to work with open-ended problems.

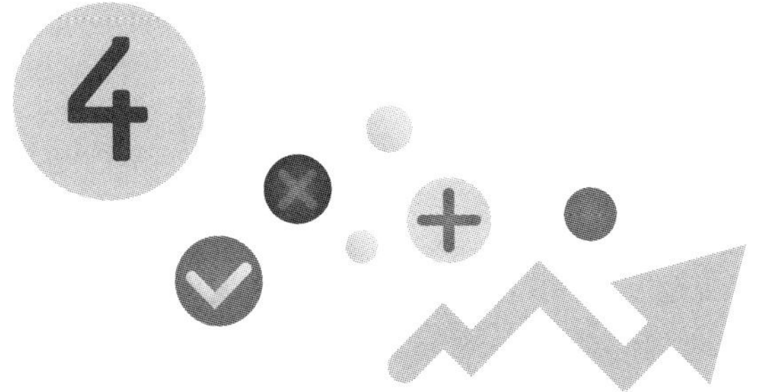

MOVING FROM ASSESSING WHAT STUDENTS KNOW TO ELICITING HOW STUDENTS UNDERSTAND

Instead of using technology as a tool for assessment *of* mathematical learning, what if we leverage technology as a tool to assess *for* learning?

THIS CHAPTER DESCRIBES two geometry classes where students are learning about trigonometric ratios. Both cases include technology within the lessons–pay attention to how the use of technology supports the teaching of math. At the beginning of each case, take a look at the ISTE Standards and math standards in your state to see how the two cases align with these expectations; later, compare with the alignment at the end of the chapter. Once you have read and reflected on the two cases, read what research has to say about two big ideas: *Technology as an Assessment Tool* and *Leveraging Students' Mathematical Understanding*. Consider how that connects with what you noticed and wondered. Finally, consider your own classroom as you contemplate the recommendations for practice.

Technology as an Assessment Tool

The U.S. Department of Education's Office of Educational Technology sets the goal: At all levels, our education system will leverage the power of technology to measure what matters and use assessment data to improve learning. Assessment helps us measure and respond to what students do and do not understand. Technology can allow us to do so more efficiently. From the early days of Scantron machines that enabled quick scoring of multiple-choice assessment items to computerized adaptive assessment, technology continues to provide increasingly sophisticated assessment tools. Many online programs now offer instantaneous feedback for students and voluminous amounts of assessment data on teacher dashboards. Although these summative measures can be helpful for many purposes, it is also important to acknowledge the potential of technology to formatively assess students to inform more in-the-moment decision making. Using technology in ways that reveal more nuanced information about how students understand math enables more responsive teaching and meaningful learning.

Leveraging Students' Mathematical Understanding

Assessment is more than grading how many answers students get right and wrong. Good classroom assessment practices elicit students' mathematical understanding— what they know and how they know it. Posing questions that elicit common misconceptions or reasoning strategies and providing students with opportunities to demonstrate their understanding in a variety of ways allows teachers better access to interpret and leverage student thinking. Technology can be a useful tool for making student thinking more visible. Once teachers have a better sense of what students know, they can adapt math instruction to more equitably improve learning.

In the following case, Mr. Simone's geometry class is learning about trigonometric ratios in right triangles. He integrates technology into the lesson as a way to assess student work. As you read this case, consider the effectiveness of technology and assessment practices during the lesson.

✔ CASE 4.1

Mr. Simone's Geometry Lesson: Trigonometric Ratios

OBJECTIVES

* Find trigonometric ratios in right triangles.

Mr. Simone is teaching a lesson about trigonometric ratios in right triangles in his geometry class. He knows that some students are already familiar with some of the ideas in the lesson. His challenge will be to keep those students engaged in a lesson that also addresses the needs of students who are new to trigonometric ratios. He decides to use a YouTube video to introduce trigonometric ratios. The video includes a SOHCAHTOA song. He thinks students will find the song amusing and it will also help them memorize the trigonometric ratios.

After the SOHCAHTOA song and video, Mr. Simone projects Geogebra (www.geogebra.org/graphing) from his computer onto the whiteboard (as shown in Figure 4.1). He previously constructed a right triangle that he shows to students.

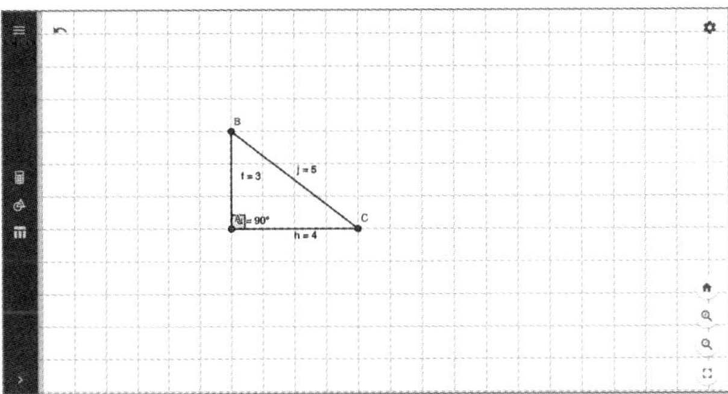

Figure 4.1 Finding ratios in a right triangle.

He randomly calls on students to take turns identifying the sine, cosine, and tangent of angles C and B. With each ratio, Mr. Simone asks the students to identify the ratio (e.g., sin C is the ratio of opposite, side f, over hypotenuse, side j). Once the ratios have all been identified, he drags points B and C to create a new right triangle with side lengths 5, 12, and 13. Mr. Simone continues to call on students to find the trigonometric ratios for angles C and B of the new triangle.

Mr. Simone divides students into two groups, and writes the homework assignment on the board. He tells the left side of the room they can get started on their homework. He asks the right side to get laptops from the shelf in the back of the room. He asks them to log into Google Classroom where he's assigned some Khan Academy practice exercises. After about ten minutes, he switches groups so all students get a chance to do the online exercises and some time to get started on homework. Although he does not have enough laptops for every student, this arrangement allows him to use online assessments for everyone. When he reviews the assessment data, he's happy to see that students performed very well at finding trigonometric ratios in right triangles. Although it took some students a few tries, they ended up getting all of the problems correct in the end.

The following day, as a warm-up, Mr. Simone displays a right triangle with side lengths 4, 8, and 8.94. He asks students to write down the sine, cosine, and tangent ratios for the triangle. Because the assessment results from the previous day were nearly perfect, he is discouraged to see that many students are writing down the wrong ratios or attempting to find trigonometric ratios for the right angle of the given triangle. He will spend time reteaching trigonometric ratios in triangles.

Reflection Questions

First consider Mr. Simone's use of technology in this lesson. He selected technologies to keep his students engaged in learning about the lesson objectives.

- Would you consider this a technology-rich lesson? Why or why not?

- What was the purpose of Mr. Simone's technology use in this lesson?

- How did Mr. Simone's integration of technology advance the teaching and learning of math in this lesson?

- What were he and/or the students able to do with technology that was different from or better than what could have been done without technology?

- How did Mr. Simone use technology as an assessment tool?

Now, consider the math teaching practices in Mr. Simone's lesson.

- What were Mr. Simone's goals for this math lesson?

- To what extent did students have equitable access to learn and demonstrate their understanding in this lesson?

- Overall, what strengths do you see in this lesson? What opportunities do you notice?

- How did Mr. Simone elicit and build upon students' mathematical thinking?

- Why do you think some students had trouble identifying trigonometric ratios even though they performed well on the previous day's assessment?

Ms. Davis's geometry class is also learning about trigonometric ratios in right triangles. As you read about Ms. Davis's lesson, consider how she integrates technology into the lesson and her mathematical teaching practices. How does she use technology as an assessment tool? To what extent does she leverage students' understanding to improve learning in the lesson?

 **CASE 4.2**

Ms. Davis's Geometry Lesson: Trigonometric Ratios

OBJECTIVE
- Find trigonometric ratios in right triangles.

Ms. Davis's geometry class will be learning to find trigonometric ratios in right triangles. Some of her students have had prior experiences learning about trigonometric ratios, but she expects this will be an introduction for much of the class. Ms. Davis has used Google Slides and Pear Deck to prepare an interactive slideshow for today's class. She will project her slides on the whiteboard, and students will work with partners on laptops to interact with the slides she's prepared.

Students in Ms. Davis's class are seated at tables with two students per table. At the beginning of class, she asks each pair to grab a laptop and go to Google Classroom where she's shared the interactive slides. The students are accustomed to using laptops during class and because there are only a limited number of devices, they are also accustomed to working cooperatively on the laptops. Students open the slides to follow along and participate in the lesson.

She begins the class by showing a slide with a right triangle (see Figure 4.2). Ms. Davis asks students to brainstorm with their partner all of the things they know, or can identify, in a right triangle. After a couple of minutes, she asks them to share their ideas. They share things such as, "It always has a right angle," and, "You can use the Pythagorean Theorem to find sides on right triangles." She probes a little deeper to see what students remember about the Pythagorean Theorem and finds that the most common thing students remember is the formula.

Ms. Davis points at the slide projected on the whiteboard. She asks students how they could label the right triangle. After a bit of wait time, she invites a student to label the triangle on the board. The student labels the three vertices A, B, and C. She then invites another student to label the sides of the triangle. That student labels the sides a, b, and c, and Ms. Davis asks if everyone agrees with the labels. Some students do not and suggest that each side should be opposite of the angle with the same letter. Ms. Davis invites another student to update the labels on the board. She again asks if everyone agrees, and there seems to be consensus at this point.

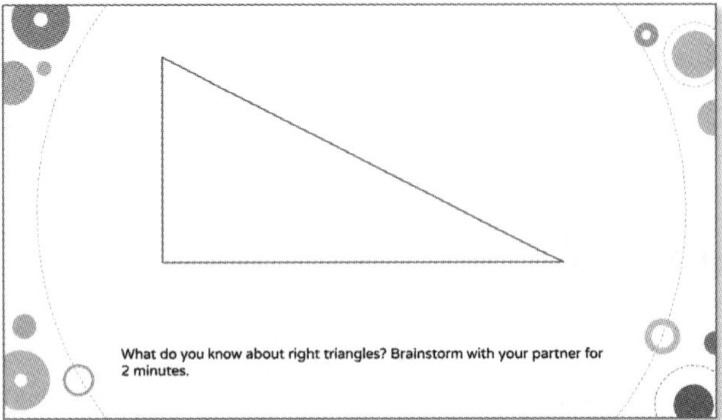

Figure 4.2 Brainstorming about right triangles

Now Ms. Davis introduces the new lesson topic: finding trigonometric ratios in right triangles. She begins with a slide to elicit students' definitions of ratio. Students type their responses onto the slide, and Ms. Davis is able to see their responses. Student definitions include such things as, "a fraction," "it's like a proportion," and, "it's a comparison of two numbers like on Twitter when someone gets ratioed." She decides to build on the last definition because it both highlights the relationship between two quantities, and connects to students' lives outside the classroom. She displays the definition to the class, and asks what it means to get ratioed on Twitter. Some students giggle and respond, "It's when someone posts something that people don't like very much, and so they get more replies than retweets and likes."

Ms. Davis follows up, "Ok, so it's a comparison between the number of replies and the number of likes or retweets? That makes sense, because in math a ratio also compares two quantities. The ratios we're talking about today are trigonometric ratios, and we are going to identify ratios in right triangles." She displays a slide (shown in Figure 4.3) with a right triangle and descriptions of sine, cosine, and tangent ratios.

She asks students if they want to find the trig ratios for angle A, which sides are the opposite, adjacent, and hypotenuse. She calls on a student who has not yet spoken up in class, and the student correctly labels a = opposite, b = adjacent, and c = hypotenuse. Then she calls on three more students to write the ratios for sin A, cos A, and tan A. She asks how the ratios would be different if they were finding sin B, cos B, and tan B. The class agrees that "b" would become the opposite side, and "a" would become the adjacent side.

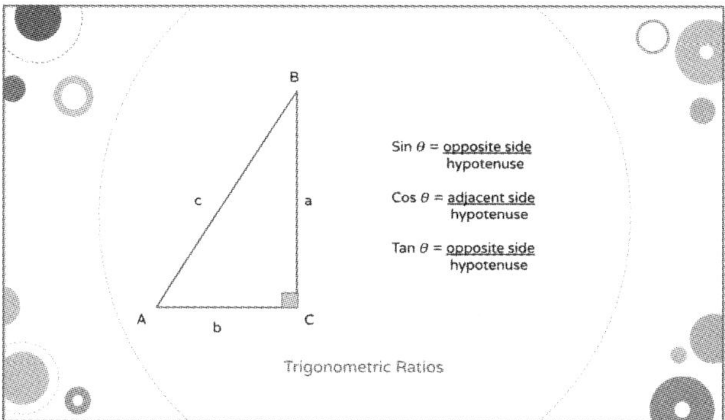

Figure 4.3 Sine, cosine, and tangent ratios.

The next part of the lesson asks students to find trig ratios in a triangle with side length measurements provided (see Figure 4.4). Students work with their partners to find the ratios and record them on the interactive slides.

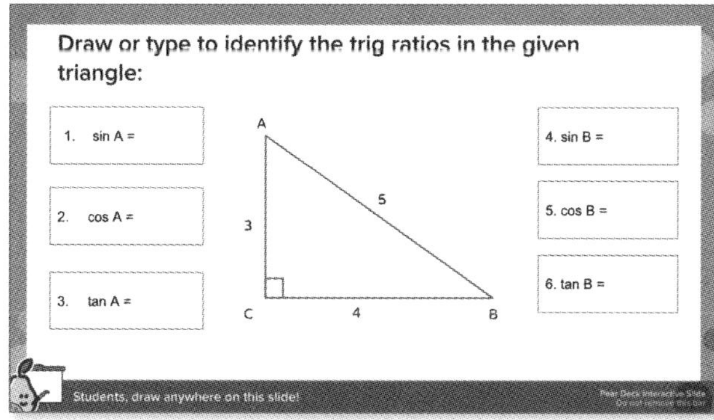

Figure 4.4 Identifying trigonometric ratios.

While the students work, Ms. Davis circulates around the room observing students, answering questions (e.g., Do I need to divide the numbers and write it as a decimal? Are we doing this right?), and checking student responses on the teacher dashboard she has displayed on her personal iPad. She notices that a few students are still confusing the sides, but most have written correct answers for all the ratios. She chooses one of the correct responses to display on the board and invites students to ask questions of their peers, but no one does.

Ms. Davis wants students to realize that the trigonometric ratios for a given angle are the same regardless of the size of the triangle. The next slide includes a link to an interactive Geogebra activity. She asks students to use the sliders to adjust the size of the triangle and make conjectures about trig ratios and triangle side lengths for similar triangles. After students have had a few minutes to explore, she asks what they notice. One student volunteers, "As long as the angle stays the same, the sides can change and the top and bottom of the ratio will change. But what it equals will stay the same." After inviting another student to explain this in her own words, Ms. Davis confirms that, by similarity, the trigonometric ratios remain the same for a fixed angle, even if the side lengths of the triangle change. This means that the sin 30 is the same whether the 30 degree angle is in a tiny right triangle or a gigantic right triangle.

To check for understanding, Ms. Davis advances to the next interactive slide (shown in Figure 4.5). The slide shows an image of two similar right triangles with their angle and side measures labelled. Students are asked to drag a dot to indicate whether they think the sine of the smaller triangle is greater than, equal to, or less than the sine of the larger triangle.

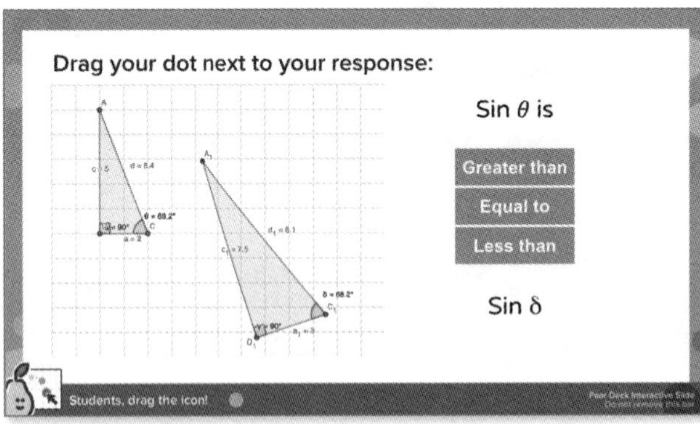

Figure 4.5   Comparing sine ratios.

At a quick glance, Ms. Davis notices that several groups indicated the sine of the angle in the smaller triangle will be less than the sine of the corresponding angle in the larger triangle. She anticipated that students might have difficulties with this idea and so prepared a slide to address this misconception. She advances to the next slide, which shows two similar triangles, and asks students to determine the cosine of a pair of corresponding angles (see Figure 4.6). She monitors as students work with their partners to set up the ratios and simplify their answers—most in decimal form. All of the students eventually find that the cosine of angles A and A'—both simplify to 12/13 or 0.923. This challenges the misconception that was revealed in the interactive slide and reinforces the idea that the trigonometric ratios of corresponding angles in similar triangles are equal.

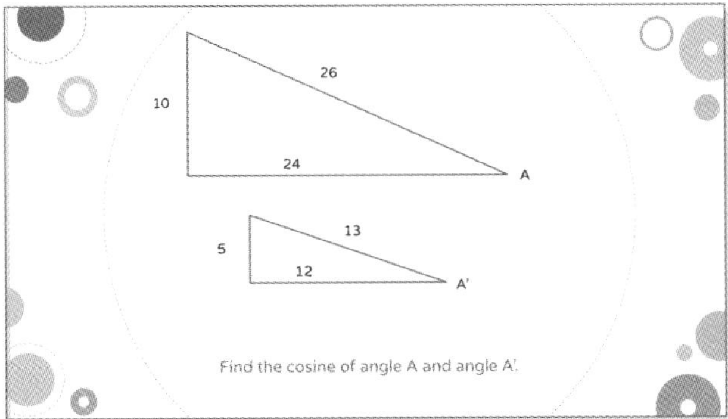

Figure 4.6 Finding the cosine of corresponding angles.

To finish the lesson, Ms. Davis divides the class in half. She asks one half to work individually on the laptops to complete Khan Academy exercises about trigonometric ratios in right triangles. The other half of the class is to use their smartphones to create short videos of themselves explaining and finding sine, cosine, and tangent ratios in two triangles Ms. Davis has projected on the board. After about ten minutes, the students switch so all have a chance to do the individual online assessment and to create a video of themselves. The scores for online practice exercises are accessible on Ms. Davis's Khan Academy teacher dashboard. She asks students to share their videos with her through Google Classroom (and turn in their corresponding work). She will review videos to assess and understand how students are thinking about the problems, and to identify where they are still making errors so she can address lingering misconceptions during the next class.

Reflection Questions

Now that you've read about Ms. Davis's lesson, think about her technology use. She selected technologies to engage and assess her students.

- Would you consider this a technology-rich lesson? Why or why not?

- What was the specific purpose of Ms. Davis's technology use in this lesson?

- How did Ms. Davis's integration of technology advance the teaching and learning in this math lesson?

- What were she and/or the students able to do with technology that was different from or better than what could have been done without technology?

- How did Ms. Davis use technology as an assessment tool?

Now, consider the math teaching practices in her lesson.

- What were Ms. Davis's goals for this math lesson?

- To what extent did students have equitable access to learn and demonstrate their understanding in this lesson?

- Overall, what strengths do you see in this lesson? What opportunities do you notice?

- How did Ms. Davis elicit and build upon students' mathematical thinking?

● ● ● ●

What Does the Research Say?

The following research supports the use of technology as an assessment tool:

- The U.S. Department of Education's Office of Educational Technology suggests that the transition from pencil-paper to digital assessments will enable a number of shifts. The shifts that technology makes possible include embedding assessment within instead of after learning, incorporating universal design principles for increased accessibility, enabling adaptive rather than fixed assessment pathways, providing real-time machine feedback rather than delayed teacher feedback, and allowing multimedia assessment items rather than generic multiple choice.

- Technology provides assessment data that was previously inaccessible to educators, parents, and students. In fact, technology has given rise to entirely new fields such as learning analytics and data mining. Many programs now offer teachers (and parents or students) dashboards of data, summarizing potentially relevant assessment information in a single snapshot. However, leveraging voluminous amounts of data requires expanded data literacy on the part of teachers. "Big data" has also given rise to new ethical concerns about privacy. Studies indicate that making assessment data more accessible to teachers can lead to better differentiation for students' individual needs and more responsive teaching. Using technology as an assessment tool offers affordances and emerging challenges for educators and new questions for researchers.

- Assessment is an ongoing focus in K–12 education and technology plays an increasing role. The use of technology as a high-stakes assessment tool makes voluminous amounts of data available for analysis and data-driven decision making. This has coincided with high-stakes assessment policy requirements since the No Child Left Behind Act of 2001. Many schools and states are transitioning to computer-based high-stakes assessments in math and other subject areas.

- Computer-based testing affords greater efficiency for schools and stakeholders. On the other hand, it can exacerbate inequities that already exist with regard to high-stakes testing. In order to implement computer-based testing, schools must have access to hardware, software, and digital infrastructure for all students. Computer-based tests must also attend to the needs of bilingual learners and special education populations.

The following research addresses leveraging students' mathematical understanding:

- While high-stakes summative assessment has driven policy in math education, much research has focused on formative classroom assessment. The National Mathematics Advisory Panel (2008) found, "teachers' regular use of formative assessment improves their students' learning" (p. xxiii). A positive association between formative assessment and improved student learning outcomes has been documented in multiple studies (e.g., Black and Wiliam, 1998a, 1998b; Hattie, 2009; Popham, 2008). Whereas summative assessments measure students' learning OF math, formative assessments focus on data and feedback FOR learning. By eliciting what students know and can do during a lesson, teachers can make instructional decisions to adapt to and better address students' learning needs (Leahy, Lyon, Thompson, & William, 2005; Wiliam, 2011).

- Eliciting and interpreting students' mathematical thinking allows teachers to appropriately respond and build upon student ideas. Multiple studies in math education focus on professional noticing of children's mathematical thinking, which includes: "a) attending to children's strategies, (b) interpreting children's understandings, and (c) deciding how to respond on the basis of children's understandings" (Jacobs, Lamb, & Philipp, 2010, p. 169). What teachers notice and attend to can have a significant impact on students' learning experiences.

- Assessing math means more than determining if answers are right or wrong. Recognizing misconceptions, error patterns, and difficulties allows teachers to diagnose and address incorrect or incomplete ideas early, before students practice and internalize them (e.g., NCTM, 2014; Schifter, 2001; Swan, 2001). To do so, teachers can design questions and tasks that purposefully elicit common errors and misconceptions (e.g., Bray, 2013; Swan, 2001). Incorporating a variety of assessment strategies also gives students an opportunity to demonstrate what and how they know, not just whether their answer is correct or not. Integrating formative assessment that notices and attends to student reasoning, including misconceptions, is a crucial component of effective math teaching practice.

Reflecting on Technology in Math Teaching

Table 4.1 Use of Technology in the Cases of Mr. Simone and Ms. Davis

	The Case of Mr. Simone	**The Case of Ms. Davis**
What technology is used?	Teacher computer and projector, shared student computers, Geogebra, and Khan Academy practice exercises online	Teacher computer, iPad, and projector; shared student computers; Pear Deck/Google Slides; Google Classroom; students' smartphones; Geogebra; and Khan Academy practice exercises online
What math is emphasized?	Find trigonometric ratios in right triangles.	Find trigonometric ratios in right triangles. Recognize that ratios of a given angle do not change with side lengths of similar triangles.
How is the lesson launched?	Mr. Simone shows a sing-along video about trigonometric ratios to begin the lesson.	Ms. Davis displays a right triangle, and asks students what they know and remember about right triangles.
Who is doing the math in this lesson?	Students identify trigonometric ratios in a whole-group setting using an image of a right triangle in Geogebra. Students work individually on homework and online practice exercises.	Students work in whole-group and pairs to identify and compare trigonometric ratios. They individually create videos to show their work for two triangles, and complete online practice exercises.
When and how is technology used in the lesson?	The beginning of the lesson is conveyed with a projected teacher device. The end of the lesson includes computers for half of the class at a time.	The beginning of the lesson is conveyed through interactive slides using a teacher device and shared student laptops. The end of the lesson includes laptops and students' smartphones used for individual assessment.

A possible perspective for comparing Mr. Simone's and Ms. Davis's technology use in these lessons might be to ask: *"How is technology used to assess students' mathematical understanding?"* Both teachers use technology in multiple ways throughout the lessons. While Mr. Simone leverages shared student devices for individual online assessments at the end of the lesson, Ms. Davis incorporates formative assessment in interactive slides during the lesson as well as individual online assessment on devices at the end of the lesson. She designed tasks to elicit students' misconceptions about right triangles and trigonometric ratios, and addressed those misconceptions through an activity that involved finding and comparing ratios in two similar triangles. Mr. Simone used assessment as a way to gauge what students had learned, whereas Ms. Davis used assessment as a way to guide and inform her teaching and, in turn, student learning.

We can also examine how technology contributed to equitable math learning experiences for all students in each class. Both lessons enabled students to participate in math discussion with the whole group and in small groups. Furthermore, all students in both classes had an opportunity to interact with technology. Both lessons included visual representations, verbal descriptions, and symbolic notation. Ms. Davis's varied forms of assessment at the end of the lesson enabled each student to demonstrate their understanding in multiple ways.

Recommendations for Practice

This chapter began with the question: *Instead of using technology as a tool for assessment OF mathematical learning, what if we leverage technology as a tool to assess FOR learning?* Classroom cases of Mr. Simone and Ms. Davis address this question. Whereas Mr. Simone uses technology-based assessment to find out what students do or don't know, Ms. Davis leverages technology for formative assessment to reveal misconceptions and inform her teaching during the lesson. Here are three practical suggestions for using technology as both a formative and summative assessment tool in your classroom.

1. Use technology to elicit what students know and understand during a lesson.

Interactive features through tools such as Pear Deck and Desmos allow teachers to pose strategic questions and gauge student understanding within lessons. Other tools include clicker devices (or apps) and the Plickers app, through which a single teacher device can quickly summarize responses from cards that students display. Both options allow teachers to pose multiple-choice questions and quickly display summaries of students' responses. Such options are anonymous and could be used to highlight common misconceptions in a way that might be more comfortable for students and teachers who are just beginning to leverage errors as part of learning.

2. Use technology to document not only students' products, but also their processes.

You can capture students' authentic work and display it for class discussion using technologies common in many classrooms (e.g., document camera, cell phone/tablet/camera, scanner, and screenshots). Using technology to document student work opens new possibilities for how they could show their work, potentially incorporating physical or virtual manipulatives, drawings, or visual models. In this way, you can rely on a broader array of evidence when assessing student work.

In addition to tools that capture the results of student work, technology also offers exciting opportunities to capture strategies and processes. Screencasting tools allow students to record their voice and writing as they solve problems. Video and audio tools can be used in a similar fashion. In a classroom with many students and only one teacher, technology tools can provide a window into students' mathematical thought processes that might otherwise be accessible only through one-on-one interactions.

3. Use data conveyed in teacher dashboards to inform your instruction.

Many popular platforms such as IXL, Khan Academy, and curriculum-based digital resources provide voluminous amounts of student assessment data in teacher dashboards. Take a closer look at what this data tells you about student understanding. Beyond how many exercises students get right or wrong, are multiple students missing the same question or giving the same incorrect answer? If so, this could indicate a shared misconception. Are some students getting perfect scores only by taking many attempts? This could be a sign that students are using immediate feedback to guess until they solve problems correctly, regardless of their actual understanding. Are some students correctly solving all the problems very quickly? Consider more appropriately challenging material. Learning to effectively use teacher dashboard data to inform your teaching is a way that technology can support assessment for learning.

Connecting Cases with Standards

In this chapter, the cases of Mr. Simone and Ms. Davis illustrate two approaches to technology-enabled assessment in a lesson on finding trigonometric ratios in right triangles. The standards identified below indicate alignment with Common Core State Standards for Mathematics and ISTE Standards for Students and for Educators. You might also consider alignment with math standards in your state or district, as well as ISTE Standards for Administrators and forCoaches.

Math Content Standard:

CCSS.MATH.CONTENT.HSG.SRT.C.6. Understand that by similarity, side ratios in right triangles are properties of the angles in the triangle, leading to definitions of trigonometric ratios for acute angles.

Mathematical Practice Standards

- Use appropriate tools strategically

- Attend to precision

- Look for and make use of structure

ISTE Standards for Educators

5a. Use technology to create, adapt and personalize learning experiences that foster independent learning and accommodate learner differences and needs.

5b. Design authentic learning activities that align with content area standards and use digital tools and resources to maximize active, deep learning.

5c. Explore and apply instructional design principles to create innovative digital learning environments that engage and support learning.

6a. Foster a culture where students take ownership of their learning goals and outcomes in both independent and group settings.

6b. Manage the use of technology and student learning strategies in digital platforms, virtual environments, hands-on makerspaces or in the field.

6d. Model and nurture creativity and creative expression to communicate ideas, knowledge or connections.

7a. Provide alternative ways for students to demonstrate competency and reflect on their learning using technology.

7b. Use technology to design and implement a variety of formative and summative assessments that accommodate learner needs, provide timely feedback to students and inform instruction.

7c. Use assessment data to guide progress and communicate with students, parents and education stakeholders to build student self-direction.

ISTE Standards for Students

1c. Students use technology to seek feedback that informs and improves their practice and to demonstrate their learning in a variety of ways.

6c. Students communicate complex ideas clearly and effectively by creating or using a variety of digital objects such as visualizations, models or simulations.

MOVING FROM TEACHER-CENTERED TO STUDENT-CENTERED INSTRUCTION

Instead of teacher-centered instruction in math, what if
we used technology as a representational tool to support
more student-centered learning experiences?

IN THIS CHAPTER, you will find two cases that take place during a Grade 6 Data and Statistics unit. Teachers in both cases utilize technology as part of their lessons on box plots, but you will notice some big differences between the two. After you read each case, consider how the lesson aligns with math content and process standards and technology standards for students and/or educators. You could compare your ideas with the alignment at the end of the chapter. After each case, take time to reflect and, if you have the opportunity, discuss with others. Once you've had a chance to read and think carefully about the similarities and differences between the two cases, read the summary of what research has to say about: *Technology as a Representational Tool* and *Empowering Student-Driven Mathematics*. Consider how the cases and research connect with your own practice as well as the recommendations for practice toward the end of the chapter.

Technology as a Representational Tool

Teachers frequently use technology to plan and deliver math lessons. Slides and presentation tools (e.g., PowerPoint, Prezi, Google Slides) are often used in college and K–12 classrooms, and some textbook publishers include slides with their math curriculum. Slides can be useful ways to organize and convey information, but traditional slides are demonstrative in nature and display only static representations. Digital technologies allow us to go beyond demonstration, enabling interactivity among students, teachers, and dynamic mathematical representations. Rather than using technology to show or tell students about a mathematical idea, interactive tools allow your students to be more participatory in the learning experience and to connect among dynamic mathematical representations.

Empowering Student-Driven Math

Math can empower students to investigate, understand, and even change the world around them. Knowing and understanding math is essential for school, college, and career. Math can also be a useful tool for analyzing issues that are important in students' lives and in society at large. Student-centered math teaching supports the development of positive mathematical identities by positioning all students as capable mathematicians. Furthermore, teaching that leverages authentic contexts, including problems that relate to students' lives, empowers students for not only important math, but also other subject areas and broader societal issues.

In the following case, Ms. Keys's class is learning to create and use box plots. She knows that technology allows a lot of access to real-world data and wants to use that information in this lesson. As you read this case, consider how technology is used for teaching and learning, and ways in which this lesson is teacher- or student-centered.

 CASE 5.1

Ms. Keys's Grade 6 Lesson: Box Plots

OBJECTIVES

- Display numerical data in a box plot.
- Use measures of center and variation to interpret data in a box plot.

Ms. Keys is teaching a lesson about creating and using box plots for data. Students should have learned about other types of data and representations in previous grades, and have recently learned how to find measures of center and variation including mean, median, mode, and range. But she wants to review in case some students did not understand or do not remember. Her goal is for students to access a data set online to make a box plot and then answer questions about it. She wants to use real-world data and, because there has been some extreme weather in their area recently, she decides to use annual precipitation data she finds online.

Sixth graders in Ms. Keys's school switch classes for math and she has the so-called "middle" group of students who tend to score "proficient" on their state math assessments. As her math group enters the classroom, she displays a warm-up word problem on the whiteboard (a logic puzzle about buckets of water) for students to solve as she collects homework. Once this routine is complete, she begins the day's lesson by displaying and saying the lesson objectives and asking students what kinds of graphs they remember. Students suggest such things as pie graphs, bar graphs, and pictographs; Ms. Keys explains that a box plot is another kind of graph that can be used to represent data and proceeds with subsequent slides that show how box plots are set up and labelled.

Ms. Keys reads the slides aloud, sometimes inviting students to read them, and she adds some additional explanation to help students understand what she wants them to know. As she explains each part of the box plot (units, labels, title, five-number summary), she demonstrates how to create a box plot using a table of rainfall totals she found online. She calls on students who raise their hands to identify the minimum, maximum, median, and quartiles. For each of the numbers, Ms. Keys shows where the number is represented on a box plot.

After using the slides to explain and demonstrate how to create a box plot, Ms. Keys wants the class to make one together. This time she hands out a worksheet with data about local annual snowfall from the last 15 years and projects the Number Line app from Math Learning Center (apps.mathlearningcenter.org/number-line) on the board. She adjusts the labels and scrolls until the numbers show the range that fits the data.

She asks students to recreate the box plot on their worksheets as the class works together. Students take turns coming to the board and drawing lines to create a box plot that represents the snowfall data Ms. Keys has provided. At the end of this activity, it appears that most students are catching on, so she decides to ask some questions about the box plot they created together. (The same questions are on their worksheet.) The questions include: What is the range of snowfall amounts during this timeframe? What is the median amount of snowfall during this timeframe? Can you use the graph to determine the total snowfall over the last 15 years? Ms. Keys gives students time to work and calls on volunteers to explain how they found their answers. She expects the last question to be challenging for many students, so she calls on a student who is usually successful.

After the whole-group instruction, Ms. Keys asks students to flip over their worksheets and work on the back side individually. The worksheet includes a chart to fill in the average annual snowfall for twelve cities chosen by the student. She tells students they can use one of the classroom tablets to look up the information they need. She prepared QR codes from several websites with historical weather data. Students are required to identify annual snowfall data for each city, find the five-number summary (minimum, maximum, median, upper and lower quartiles), determine a scale, and create a box plot to display the data. She appreciates that the activity requires students to use internet resources to find authentic data. The questions on the worksheet are similar to those she asked during the whole-class activity: What is the difference between the greatest snowfall amount and the least snowfall amount? How many cities had annual snowfall above 40 inches? What is the range of snowfall for all the cities you selected?

She knows that not all students have access to a computer at home to look up the information they need, so she encourages them to find their snowfall data during class time and finish the questions outside of class as homework.

Reflection Questions

First, consider how Ms. Keys used technology in this lesson. She used technology to display content on slides, to project a number line and create a box plot, and for students to access authentic data online.

- Would you consider this a technology-rich lesson? Why or why not?

- How did Ms. Keys's integration of technology advance the teaching and learning in this math lesson?

- To what extent did technology empower students as math learners?

- How did Ms. Keys use technology as a representational tool?

Now, consider the math teaching practices in Ms. Keys's lesson.

- What were Ms. Keys's goals for this math lesson?

- To what extent did students have equitable access to learn and demonstrate their understanding in this lesson?

- Overall, what strengths do you see in this lesson? What opportunities do you notice?

- Would you categorize this lesson as more teacher-centered, or more student-centered? Why?

- What mathematical challenges and errors would you anticipate students might experience in this lesson?

Ms. Young's class is also learning about box plots and measures of center. The next case describes how she integrates technology into her lesson and her math teaching practices. Consider how she uses technology as a representational tool. Is the lesson more teacher-centered or student-centered?

⊘ CASE 5.2

Ms. Young's Grade 6 Lesson: Box Plots

OBJECTIVES

- Display numerical data in a box plot.

- Use measures of center and variation to interpret data in a box plot.

Ms. Young teaches in a mountainous rural area. Her class is learning about measures of center and representing numerical data in various graphs. They have also been learning about analyzing and interpreting data on natural hazards (NGSS MS-ESS3-2). For today's lesson, Ms. Young has decided to expand the procedural treatment of box plots in her math textbook and will instead integrate these two ideas along with a connection to their local community, which recently experienced nearby wildfires. In this way, the class can use math as a tool to help students understand science and the world around them. Several students in the class have smartphones or tablets and she has some classroom tablets as well. They'll use their devices in today's lesson.

For the past few weeks, students have been learning about earth and human activity in science, with particular focus on phenomena related to natural hazards such as earthquakes, volcanoes, severe weather events, and forest fires. Their science lessons have focused on types of natural hazards, as well as measuring, monitoring, and predicting natural hazards. Up until this point, the hazards the class has discussed (e.g., volcanoes, earthquakes, hurricanes, floods) rarely take place in their mountainous region. However, yesterday's science lesson included wildfires, which occur somewhat frequently in surrounding areas. In fact, a wildfire burned many acres in the county where the school is located, some of it dangerously near students' homes. During that lesson, one student shared his grandfather's remark that, "Fires like this hardly ever happened fifty years ago, but these days it seems like there's fires every other year." Ms. Young decided to use today's math lesson about box plots to provide students an opportunity to delve deeper into data about wildfires.

To begin today's lesson, Ms. Young displays the interactive Number Line app from Math Learning Center on the board (apps.mathlearningcenter.org/number-line), showing a number line that starts at zero and is labelled by units of one (See Figure 5.1.).

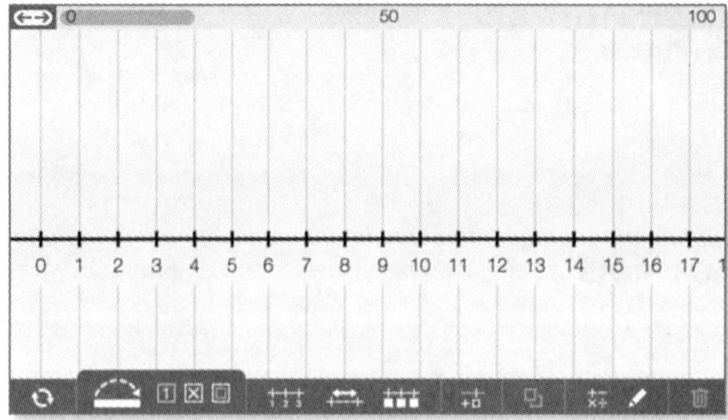

Figure 5.1   Interactive number line.

She also hands out small sticky notes and asks students to write down their number of siblings on the sticky note and place it on the board, as close as they can to number on their paper.

Most students place their sticky notes between one and three, and some indicate no siblings or up to six siblings. The resulting graph resembles a line plot.

Referring to the line plot, Ms. Young asks whether the graph represents the data in a useful way. The class agrees that it shows most students have one, two, or three siblings. She asks if it would be useful to know the mode of this data and students agree it would. She then asks if they can tell the median number of siblings from this graph. After some consideration and brief discussion, they decide that the graph does not show the median number of siblings, but that they could figure it out. Before she invites the class to show how they would find the median, she asks them what the minimum and maximum number of siblings is in their data set. They identify zero and six, and Ms. Young draws vertical lines above those numbers on the board. She then encourages students to use the sticky notes on the board to find the median number of siblings for their class. During this discussion, a student volunteer goes to the board and puts all of the sticky notes in numerical order. Ms. Young asks another student to explain how to find the median from the ordered list. The student draws a mark above the first and last sticky note and repeats the process, working her way toward the middle of the list until she only has two notes left, both of which say two. The class concludes that two is the median number of siblings.

Ms. Young then asks, "What if you wanted to find the median of the top and bottom halves of the data set?" A student explains that you could do the same thing, but just pair off values within one side of the ordered list. Ms. Young invites students to find the median of the bottom half of their data, which is one, and the top half of the data, which is three. She draws vertical lines above those numbers and asks students to discuss what each of the lines she drew represents. Students identify the minimum, maximum, median, and the medians of the top and bottom half of the data. Ms. Young introduces math vocabulary, lower quartile and upper quartile, to describe the medians of the two halves. She asks students why the median of a half might be called a "quartile." Many students seem confused, but one student suggests that they are dividing each half into halves, and half of a half is a quarter, which sounds like the word quartile. Ms. Young agrees and repeats the student's explanation.

On the board, she writes Min (Minimum) = 0, Q1 (Lower Quartile) = 1, Median = 2, Q3 (Upper Quartile) = 3, Max (Maximum) = 6, summarizing the class discussion. Ms. Young then draws horizontal lines between the quartiles to create a box and connects the box to the maximum and minimum with two more horizontal lines. She explains that the resulting graph (shown in Figure 5.2) is called a box plot.

Ms. Young asks if the class can tell what the median is by looking at this graph. They agree that they can. She asks if the graph shows how many students have two or more siblings. After some consideration and a brief discussion, the class agrees that the box plot does not show how many people gave any of the answers. Ms. Young explains that box plots are most useful for seeing the distribution of data. Finally, she asks what an appropriate title for the graph might be; the class agrees on "Number of Siblings for Students in Ms. Young's Class."

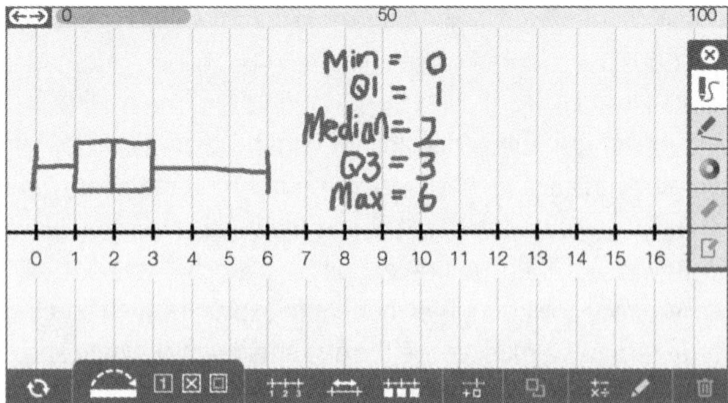

Figure 5.2 Number of siblings.

To check for understanding, Ms. Young passes out more sticky notes and asks students to repeat the activity, but this time to write how many cousins they have. She encourages students to work collaboratively as she observes and listens. The class is able to generate the box plot represented in Figure 5.3.

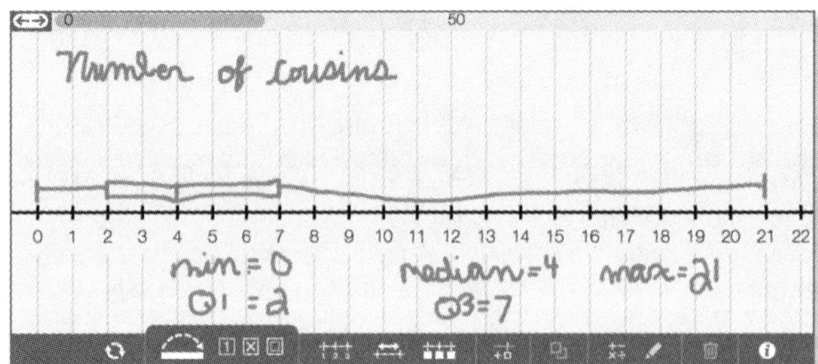

Figure 5.3 Number of cousins.

Ms. Young compliments the class on their teamwork and the box plot they created. She asks how this box plot compares to the one about siblings. Students respond using terms such as "bigger" and "stretched out further." Ms. Young affirms their ideas and offers that the graphs show that the distributions of the data are different. She asks students to find the range of the cousin data and sibling data (students are familiar with finding range of data sets from a previous lesson). Then she asks them what information the two graphs could convey to someone who wasn't in their class. Students suggest that the graphs show that overall they have fewer siblings than cousins, and that the numbers of cousins that people have is a bigger range than the number of siblings. The box plot, discussion, and participation by all students indicate to Ms. Young that the class understands how to make and interpret box plots, so she moves on to the next activity: applying box plots to analyze data about wildfires.

During this next activity, students will have the option to use an online interactive applet to create box plots and will focus on interpreting the data representations. Ms. Young projects the website www.shodor.org/interactivate/activities/BoxPlot on the board and shows students how to use the online tool using a provided data set about Horsepower of Cars. Because students will be entering data they find online, she shows them how to use the My Data data set, where to enter their data, and how to update the resulting box plot. The app works better on a tablet or laptop, so she encourages students to work in groups of two or three where at least one student has a tablet or laptop.

For the class exploration, Ms. Young reminds them of the claim in science class the previous day that wildfires seem to occur more frequently in recent years. To explore this claim, the class will create box plots to show the number of wildfires and the acres burnt during different periods of time. Students are asked to access historical data from the National Interagency Fire Center at www.nifc.gov/fireInfo/fireInfo_stats_totalFires.html, which includes data dating back to 1926 (though the site cautions against comparing pre-1983 data with post-1983 data due to inconsistencies in the reporting process).

To encourage students to make sense of the data and apply box plots in useful ways, Ms. Young gives the class an open-ended exploration:

- Create two or more box plots that can help analyze and interpret data to understand whether wildfires in the U.S. have become more common in recent years.

Students must decide whether to compare acres burned or number of fires, and will need to decide on what to compare. Ms. Young wants students to realize that box plots do not show trends over time, but distributions of data. She asks students to use descriptive titles and to take a screenshot of the box plots they create. Some of the prompts she is prepared to ask students who are struggling include:

- What can you tell by looking at a box plot?

- You're supposed to make at least two box plots—what are two data sets you could compare that would help show whether or not there are more wildfires than there used to be?

- How does comparing the number of wildfires and the number of acres burned in wildfires help you understand if there are more fires than there used to be?

- What timeframes would be useful to compare?

Students work in pairs and small groups to determine which data to include in their box plots. As Ms. Young anticipated, some students begin by making a box plot for the number of fires and another for the acres burned. Another group talks about how long ago someone's grandpa might remember as they decide on a date range for their data. Many students find it challenging to choose data sets to compare for a specific purpose. Ms. Young monitors as students work, asking questions and drawing from the prompts she had prepared in anticipation of student difficulties.

As class time draws to an end, Ms. Young checks with each student group to make sure they have created useful box plots from the wildfire data. As homework, she asks students to use the data shown in their group's box plots to determine the validity of the claim that there are more wildfires now than there used to be.

To conclude the lesson, Ms. Young tells the class that they will present their box plots tomorrow and discuss what their data shows about wildfires. They will also spend time during science learning more about wildfires and technologies used to prevent and contain fires. They will also videoconference with someone from the local fire department to discuss these ideas and how they are applied in their community.

Ms. Young is pleased that not only did students represent data in box plots and use interactive tools to access and represent data, but they also strengthened their understanding of natural hazards and related it to recent catastrophic events in their local community.

Reflection Questions

Consider how Ms. Young used technology in this lesson.

- Would you consider this a technology-rich lesson? Why or why not?

- What was the specific purpose of Ms. Young's technology use in this lesson?

- To what extent did technology empower students as math learners?

- How did Ms. Young use technology a representational tool?

Consider the math teaching practices in Ms. Young's lesson.

- What were Ms. Young's goals for this math lesson? Were they achieved?

- To what extent did students have equitable access to learn and demonstrate their understanding in this lesson?

- Overall, what strengths do you see in this lesson? What opportunities do you notice?

- Would you categorize this lesson as more teacher-centered, or more student-centered? Why?

- What mathematical challenges and errors would you anticipate students might experience in this lesson?

● ● ● ●

What Does the Research Say?

The following research supports the use of technology as a representational tool:

- NCTM identifies *Use and connect mathematical representations* as one of eight effective math teaching practices. When students make connections among contextual, visual, verbal, physical, and symbolic representations (Lesh, Post, & Behr, 1987), the variety of perspectives help them deepen their understanding of mathematical concepts (Tripathi, 2008). Visual representations, in particular, can be powerful ways to expand access to emergent bilinguals and struggling learners (Fuson & Murata, 2007). Connecting among dynamic digital representations and mathematical models supports students with visualizing mathematical relationships and concepts (Roschelle et al, 2010).

- Technology-enabled dynamic representations allow users to manipulate mathematical objects, quickly explore numerous iterations or mathematical scenarios, and visualize how connected representations change and are connected. Dynamic geometry environments (DGEs) support geometric constructions that can be quickly changed through dragging points in infinitely many locations. Computer algebra systems permit students to make and test conjectures, while automating tedious and time-consuming computation and algebraic manipulation. Overall, the types of dynamic representations afforded by technology tools impact how students can visualize and interact with math and open up new opportunities for deep mathematical discussion about explorations that would be impractical or impossible with pencil and paper alone.

- When evaluating technology for use in math lessons, teachers in one study tended to associate dynamic, interactive representations with transformative technology integration, whereas static, fixed representations corresponded with integrating technology as a mere replacement

(Hughes, Thomas, & Scharber, 2006; Thomas & Edson, 2017). Teachers in the study also associated transformative technology integration with not only showing representations, but also connecting and discussing among multiple, often dynamic, representations.

The following research addresses empowering Student-Driven Math:

- The guidelines for assessment and instruction in statistics education (GAISE) (Franklin et al., 2005) offer a framework of three levels through which students progress. It is appropriate for beginning students to use data from a classroom census or simple experiment and begin to compare data from one group to another. As students transition to the second level, they begin to use data distributions as tools for analysis and acknowledge that looking beyond specific data can tell a larger story. The sixth-grade students in Ms. Young's class are beginning to engage in Level B statistical thinking. Not only are learning progressions important for statistical understanding, understanding levels of geometric thought (Burger & Shaughnessy, 1986; van Hiele, 1980) and learning trajectories about number and operations (Clements & Sarama, 2009) also help teachers design learning experiences that are developmentally appropriate and better meet students' needs.

- Research and discussion about teacher- and student-centered teaching date back more than a century to the reform era of John Dewey. The constructivist learning theories of Piaget and sociocultural theories of Vygotsky emphasize student-centered learning. Active construction of knowledge and building mathematical understanding through discourse centers students in the learning experience, whereas traditional, teacher-centered approaches position students as passive recipients of disciplinary knowledge. Student-centered instruction allows teachers to respond to students' needs and develop positive identities as mathematical learners.

- Math teaching that promotes equitable access for all students affirms and builds upon students' identities and contexts. "Effective teachers draw on community resources to understand how they can use contexts, culture, conditions, and language to support mathematics teaching and learning" (NCTM, 2014, p. 65; Berry & Ellis, 2013; Cross et al., 2012; Kisker et al., 2012; Moschkovich, 1999, 2011; Planas and Civil, 2013). Drawing upon culture and relevant contexts is one aspect of teaching math for social justice, an approach that can deepen students' understanding of social issues, motivate mathematical learning, and highlight math as a tool to understand the world (Gutstein & Peterson, 2013; Larson, 2017). When teachers provide equitable opportunities to use technology to solve rich mathematical problems about important contexts, all students benefit.

Reflecting on Technology in Math Teaching

As you read the cases of Ms. Keys's and Ms. Young's sixth-grade classrooms, you probably compared their teaching to one another and perhaps to your own classroom or those you have observed. Table 5.1 offers a comparative summary of some aspects of the two cases.

TABLE 5.1 Use of Technology in the Cases of Ms. Keys and Ms. Young

	The Case of Ms. Keys	The Case of Ms. Young
What technology is used?	Slides and projector, interactive number line, QR codes, online data sources	Teacher device and projector, interactive number line, student devices, online box plot applet, online data source
What math is emphasized?	Creating and interpreting box plots	Creating and interpreting box plots and making decisions about what data is appropriate for representing in a box plot
How is the lesson launched?	Ms. Keys gives a warm-up problem, states the objective, and asks students what they remember about today's topic.	Ms. Young engages students in collecting and representing data about siblings and cousins at the outset.
Who is doing the math in this lesson?	Ms. Keys shows students how to create box plots from online data, creates a box plot with student input, and then asks students to make their own plots.	Students collect data about their families and work together to choose data sets for analysis with box plots. Students create box plots as a whole group and in small groups.
When and how is technology used in the lesson?	Slides are used to convey instruction about how to make a box plot. The class uses an interactive number line as a background to create a box plot. Students access online data through digital devices.	The class uses an interactive number line to create box plots on the board. Students use personal devices to access historical wildfire data, and an interactive app to create box plots from the data.

Although the two teachers in these cases use similar technologies for teaching, one might wonder: *"How does technology help students create and understand box plots in these two lessons?"* Ms. Keys uses slides to show and tell students how to create box plots, projects a number line app for the class to create a box plot, and requires students to access online data for their homework assignment. Ms. Young, on the other hand, uses an interactive tool that allows students to focus on connections among dynamic representations rather than simple computations. Students use their own devices to access authentic data to answer a question that arose in their science class. In addition, Ms. Young uses interactive video technology to virtually connect students with professional firefighters who can offer relevant local insight into students' data-informed insights and conclusions about the science of wildfires.

Technology supported the two teachers' math teaching practices, particularly with respect to student-centeredness. Ms. Keys used a more teacher-centered approach, using technology to show students procedures for creating box plots and identifying the specific sites where students could locate the data she wanted them to plot. Ms. Keys did use authentic data to try to interest students, but they did not have an opportunity to measure or collect authentic data or interpret it in the context of their own lives and experiences. Some of the comparison questions Ms. Keys asked students made little sense in context. For instance, it was unclear why students would need, or want, to know the range of snowfall among a variety of cities. One might say that she selected a context to serve the math, but it did not always make sense in that context.

Ms. Young employed a more student-centered approach, beginning with a chance for students to collect authentic data and then compare two data sets using box plots. Throughout this lesson, students collected or used authentic data, and related their observations to themselves, what they were learning in science, and their local community. Ms. Young's students were able to not only create box plots, but also see how box plots could help make sense of data that mattered in the world around them. After the lesson, students engaged in an extended task comparing data from the box plots they created, extending their knowledge about wildfires and technologies for preventing and containing them, then talking to experts to deepen their understanding about the context. In Ms. Young's lesson, math served the context, allowing students to predict and understand the results of their experiment, the results of which contributed to further science learning.

Recommendations for Practice

We began this chapter by asking: *Instead of teacher-centered instruction in math, what if we used technology as an interactive tool to support more student-centered learning experiences?* Cases from Ms. Keys and Ms. Young's classrooms offer a sense of how that shift might look in a lesson about data. For your own classroom, consider the following recommendations for leveraging technology as an interactive tool and supporting student-centered instruction.

1. Use interactive features to engage students in mathematical exploration.

If a picture is worth a thousand words, what might be the value of an interactive tool with countless visualizations? Ms. Keys and Ms. Young used an interactive number line in their lessons. Many virtual manipulatives offer interactive features. Base ten block apps often allow one to instantaneously group and ungroup blocks, illustrating place value relationships. With dynamic geometry environments (DGEs) such as Geogebra, Cabri, or Geometer's Sketchpad, children can drag shapes to show an infinite number of versions. Sliders within DGEs allow students to visualize the impact of various parameters on graphs or shapes. For instance, what happens to the sides of a triangle when one of the angles increases or decreases? Or how does the graph of a line change when the slope goes from positive to negative? Dynamic, interactive technologies enable visualizations and potential connections across mathematical representations that are not otherwise possible with fixed images.

2. Use technology to connect students with people and contexts that are relevant to their lives.

Word problems and applications are often intended to show math in the "real world," but are those problems real and relevant for students, or are they fake and contrived? Few students will find intrinsic value in knowing the volume of a hypothetical rectangular swimming pool with a constant depth of five feet. But they might care about the volume of a raised garden bed they need to fill with soil for a school garden. Or, they could use online design tools to design a raised garden bed, and explore the cost of soil from local garden supply stores–making the math real for their lives. Technology can also be used for students to access and understand math in relation to broader social issues. Ms. Young's lesson might explore more deeply issues of climate change and how it impacts wildfires in their mountain region. Instead of solving worksheets involving proportions out of context, or in contrived contexts, students could apply proportional reasoning and access online electoral data to investigate gerrymandering of legislative districts in their state, and consider issues of representation. In this respect, student-centered teaching with technology not only empowers students to build their understanding of math, but also to discover how math can be used as a tool for understanding their world and lived experiences.

Connecting Cases with Standards

The cases of Ms. Keys and Ms. Young highlight technology as a representational tool and student-centered approaches to teaching. The standards identified below indicate alignment with Common Core State Standards for Mathematics, and ISTE Standards for Students and for Educators. You might also consider alignment with math standards in your state or district, as well as ISTE Standards for Administrators and for Coaches.

Math Content Standards

CCSS.MATH.CONTENT.6.SPB.4. Display numerical data in plots on a number line, including dot plots, histograms, and box plots.

CCSS.MATH.CONTENT.6.SPB.5.C. Summarize numerical data sets in relation to their context, such as by giving quantitative measures of center (median and/ or mean) and variability (interquartile range and/or mean absolute deviation), as well as describing any overall pattern and any striking deviations from the overall pattern with reference to the context in which the data were gathered.

Mathematical Practice Standards

- Make sense of problems and persevere in solving them.
- Construct viable arguments and critique the reasoning of others.
- Model with mathematics.
- Use appropriate tools strategically.
- Attend to precision.

ISTE Standards for Educators

3b. Establish a learning culture that promotes curiosity and critical examination of online resources and fosters digital literacy and media fluency.

4c. Use collaborative tools to expand students' authentic, real-world learning experiences by engaging virtually with experts, teams and students, locally and globally.

5b. Design authentic learning activities that align with content area standards and use digital tools and resources to maximize active, deep learning.

5c. Explore and apply instructional design principles to create innovative digital learning environments that engage and support learning.

6a. Foster a culture where students take ownership of their learning goals and outcomes in both independent and group settings.

ISTE Standards for Students

3d. Students build knowledge by actively exploring real-world issues and problems, developing ideas and theories and pursing answers and solutions.

5b. Students collect data or identify relevant data sets, use digital tools to analyze them, and represent data in various ways to facilitate problem-solving and decision-making.

6c. Students communicate complex ideas clearly and effectively by creating or using a variety of digital objects such as visualizations, models or simulations.

7b. Students use collaborative technologies to work with others, including peers, experts or community members, to examine issues and problems from multiple viewpoints.

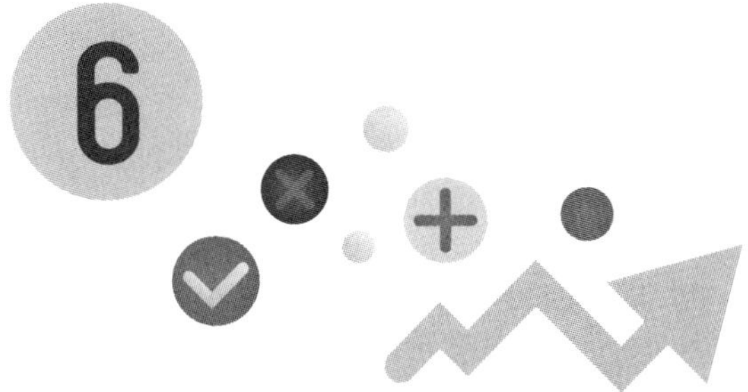

MOVING FROM TECHNOLOGY FOR ITS OWN SAKE TO TECHNOLOGY FOR RICH MATH LEARNING

Instead of using technology for its own sake, what if we used technology in the service of learning rich, interesting math?

IN THIS CHAPTER, you will get a glimpse of two seventh-grade classrooms where technology is used as part of a lesson about scale drawings. While you're reading, think about the extent to which technology is supporting math learning in these two cases. You might also examine how each of the lessons aligns with standards for math content, mathematical practices, and ISTE standards for students and educators. Compare what you find with the alignment at the end of this chapter. After reading and reflecting upon the two cases, compare your insights and connections with what research has to say about two big ideas illustrated in the cases: *Technology as an Educational Tool* and *Teaching and Learning Mathematics with Technology.*

Technology as an Educational Tool

Technology is important and worth learning about in its own right. Digital tools continue to enable innovations in school, society, and the workplace. Automation, artificial intelligence, virtual reality, and new avenues for communication and connectivity will continue to transform the world where students live and will work. It is important for students to learn about innovative technologies and to gain the technological literacy required for life in the digital age. But when, in a crowded school curriculum, can students have the opportunities needed to develop techno-logical literacy? Although mathematical thinking and learning are inextricably linked with cutting edge technologies, students and teachers do not always recognize connections between math learning and technology. Through carefully-designed instructional activities, students can develop technological skills in the context of learning math. Such an approach positions even the most cutting-edge digital tools, not as toys, but as educational tools. Using innovative technologies as educational tools aligned with standards for math learning also opens up more time and oppor-tunities for students to develop technological literacy during regular class time.

Teaching and Learning Mathematics with Technology

The NCTM Tool and Technology Principle reads: "An excellent mathematics program integrates the use of mathematical tools and technology as essential resources to help students learn and make sense of mathematical ideas, reason mathematically, and communicate their mathematical thinking" (2014, p. 78). It is not enough to integrate technology into a math class if that technology is not helping students learn, make sense, reason, and communicate about math. At the same time, technology is widely used to do math in the real world, and it is imper-ative that students learn with, and are prepared to use tools of the trade. Through strategic use of technology, students can develop deeper understanding of geom-etry, measurement, algebra, numbers, and data.

In the following case, Ms. Atwood is teaching her seventh-grade class a lesson about scale drawings. To what extent is technology used as an educational tool during her lesson? In what ways are students learning math through the use of technology?

 CASE 6.1

Ms. Atwood's Grade 7 Lesson on Scale Drawings

OBJECTIVES

* Solve problems involving scale drawings
* Reproduce a scale drawing at a different scale
* Explore new coding robots

Ms. Atwood's students recently began a geometry unit. In this lesson they'll be learning about scale drawings.

Recently, Ms. Atwood went to a conference where she learned about coding robots and heard about how other teachers were using robots to get their students really excited about learning. She was so impressed that she applied for some classroom funding to purchase a few coding robots for her students to use. Today is the first day she'll be using the robots in her class, and she's decided to incorporate them during her seventh-grade math class because math and technology are both part of STEM—a big emphasis in her school.

Ms. Atwood planned this lesson to be fairly quick because many students are already familiar with the underlying concepts. During the rest of math class, students will get a chance to use the coding robots. She will begin with a lesson from Eureka Math, her school's approved OER math curriculum. The lesson, Relating Scale Drawings to Ratios and Rates, is the first in the unit. For the sake of time, the class will skip the third example and exercise. If students need more support on these topics, they will have a chance to revisit them in subsequent lessons. She projects lesson materials on the interactive whiteboard so students can follow along and write or draw on the screen during class discussion.

The class begins with a brief opening exercise guessing images that are reductions and enlargements. In their first example of a scale drawing, Ms. Atwood introduces the term *scale drawing*, and several students contribute to a discussion about possible uses for enlarged and reduced drawings or pictures. In their second example, students compare two drawings that are proportional, but oriented differently. The class discusses the importance of positioning and identifying corresponding points in scale drawings. Students then spend time creating scale drawings of robots on grid paper. Ms. Atwood wraps up this part of the lesson by reviewing the definition of scale drawing, enlargement, reduction, and the importance of matching corresponding points in scale drawings.

Once the class is done with the more formal part of the lesson, Ms. Atwood tells students they will have a chance to use coding robots to explore ideas about scale.

Ms. Atwood shows one of the robots, shows them the Chromebook app they can use to control the robot, and demonstrates how they can trace paths on the screen that the robot will follow onto the floor. To connect with today's math lesson, she shows that the drawings they create on their screen are in one scale, but the paths the robot follows are at a different scale.

Then, she puts students in groups of four to five, and tells them they will take turns controlling the robots, within their groups. Each student will have about five minutes to explore with the robot, and each group will stay in a specific area of the classroom. Next, she gives each group a Chromebook and a robot, and directs them toward a corner of the room where they will explore for the remainder of math class. She goes from group to group, ensuring that students are engaged, on task, and taking turns appropriately.

Reflection Questions

First consider Ms. Atwood's use of technology in this lesson. She explicitly defined a technology goal, and was enthusiastic about incorporating a new tool in her math class.

- Would you consider this a technology-rich lesson? Why or why not?

- What was the purpose of Ms. Atwood's technology use in this lesson?

- How did Ms. Atwood's integration of technology advance the teaching and learning in this math lesson?

- What were she and/or the class able to do with technology that was different from or better than what could have been done without technology?

- Were there any downsides to Ms. Atwood's incorporation of technology in this lesson?

Next, consider the math teaching practices in Ms. Atwood's lesson.

- What were Ms. Atwood's goals for this math lesson?

- Would you say that this lesson exemplifies what it means to teach and learn math with technology? Why or why not?

- To what extent did students have equitable access to learn and demonstrate their understanding in this lesson?

- Overall, what strengths do you see in this lesson? What opportunities do you notice?

● ● ● ●

Mr. Smith's seventh-grade class is also learning about scale drawings. As you read about Mr. Smith's lesson, consider how he teaches math with technology. Take note of the opportunities students have to learn math through technology, and how they contribute to the lesson objectives.

 **CASE 6.2**

Mr. Smith's Grade 7 Lesson on Scale Drawings

OBJECTIVES

- Solve problems involving scale drawings
- Reproduce a scale drawing at a different scale
- Explore new coding robots

It's near the end of the school year, and Mr. Smith's class is working on a geometry unit. Today, they will learn about scale drawings and reproducing scale drawings at a different scale. In addition, students will have a chance to work with some new coding robots Mr. Smith checked out from their school's technology coach.

A couple of months ago, Mr. Smith read an article about coding in middle school classes. He was surprised to learn that students with little experience were writing programs that created on-screen animations and manipulated robots! Although he knew very little about coding himself, he wanted to know more, so he met with the school technology coordinator. The coordinator pointed him toward coding robots that can be controlled in a variety of ways. Mr. Smith began experimenting with the Sphero robots. He started at Sphero.edu where he created a program using the Draw feature. He drew paths on the screen, connected with a Sphero robot, and watched as the robot followed his paths in the real world. He also played with the Blocks programming feature where he could create programs by dragging, dropping, and connecting puzzle-piece blocks on screen. He briefly explored options within the JavaScript Wiki, but didn't feel ready to write programs using more formal programming languages.

Mr. Smith knows that his students have experience with measurement and proportional reasoning from math curriculum in prior grades and earlier this year. Because scale drawings, in some sense, apply proportional reasoning to measurement, he thinks that most students would have little trouble getting started with a scale drawing lesson. To be sure to guide his lesson and activity, he delivers a pre-assessment about scale drawings the day before he will introduce the Spheros. The entire unit will take multiple lessons, but he is confident that students have enough prior knowledge to start the unit with a scale drawing challenge involving the coding robots.

The class begins with a learnzillion.com lesson titled: What are Scaled Drawings?–adapted from the Illustrative Mathematics curriculum his school uses. Mr. Smith will use the online lesson's warm-up, first activity, and synthesis, which should take about 25 minutes. For the rest of class, students will explore scaled drawings with the Sphero robots.

Students work in pairs on Chromebooks to compare portraits of a student on a slide, and Mr. Smith uses a think-pair-share strategy to engage them in conversation about how the portraits are the same as, or different from, the original portrait, which are scaled copies, and what scale copy means. Students also interact with an applet that resizes the portraits in different ways, discussing and refining their ideas about scaled copies. Mr. Smith invites three student pairs to share their definitions of "scaled copy," and the class discusses the definitions. The class agrees to the working definition that scaled copies have the same proportions, but might be different sizes.

The class proceeds with the first activity of the lesson. They continue to work in pairs with a Chromebook and projected slides on the whiteboard. The next slide asks students to identify which versions of an original version of the letter F are scaled drawings. The versions are shown on a coordinate grid, so students have a chance to consider and discuss measurements that were not visible in the opening activity. Students work together to create different scaled copies of the letter F in an embedded applet as part of the online lesson. The class concludes this activity by sharing their online scale drawings, and engaging in a whole-class discussion about the features that scaled copies share with specific reference to the drawings students created and those from the beginning of the lesson.

Mr. Smith then explains that students will spend the rest of class exploring scaled drawings with Sphero robots. Some students have encountered Spheros in a computer class or STEM-related activities, but this will be the first encounter for more than half the class. For this reason, the activity assumes no prior experience with Sphero or Sphero.edu. Mr. Smith asks students to continue working with their partners, and creates small groups of four by assigning students to work with another pair. He takes into account the results of the pre-assessment when putting pairs together to make groups. He wants to ensure that all students in each group can work productively together, that all group members' understandings are diverse enough to invite interesting discussions, but not so disparate as to potentially leave some students out of group tasks.

Once students are in their groups, Mr. Smith projects the Sphero.edu screen on the board (see Figure 6.1) and places a robot on the floor in the front of the classroom. He then creates a program using the Draw feature, and roughly sketches a rectangle on the gridded screen. He tells students that when he presses the Start button, the robot will follow the path he drew. He instructs students to talk in their groups about how big they think the path will be.

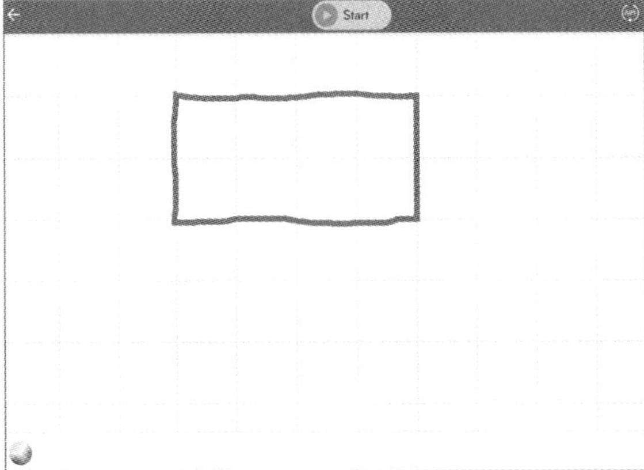

Figure 6.1   Rectangular path for Sphero.

Because the floor of their classroom is tiled, many students reason in terms of how many tiles Sphero will travel. The most popular idea is that the robot will go forward four tiles before turning and traveling two tiles. Mr. Smith reiterates this popular idea by saying, "I hear several students predicting that Sphero will travel one square floor tile for every square on the grid. Let's see if they are right!"

To test their prediction, Mr. Smith presses start, and the class watches as the Sphero robot traces a rectangle on the floor. "It looks like our prediction wasn't quite right. Now we know that the path the robot takes is a scaled version of what we see on the screen. But what we don't know yet is what that scale is. That's what you get to work on in your groups for the rest of class today. First, work together to figure out how far one on-screen grid square relates to how far Sphero travels in real life. Once you get that figured out, use this tape [holds up painter's tape] to make a path on the floor. Then draw a path in sphero.edu so that the robot follows your tape. Jace, will you please repeat the directions for this activity so everyone can hear them again?"

Jace repeats, "We have to figure out how far Sphero moves on the ground when it's supposed to go one square on the screen. Then we make a track using the tape, and draw a path on the computer for the robot to follow the tape."

Mr. Smith affirms Jace's explanation, and asks students to get started while he hands out materials: painters tape, a measuring tape, scrap paper, and individual worksheets for students to record their thinking. He encourages the groups to spread out throughout the classroom so everyone has room to work.

Mr. Smith circulates around the classroom to observe and listen in on different groups' conversations. Most of the groups are drawing lines on the screen, and using the measuring tapes to figure out how far Sphero travels to follow their lines. He visits Sabrina, Abel, Darin, and Shanna's group just as they begin creating their taped path. They have sketched the shape of a spiral-like path on their worksheet, and are deciding how big it should be.

Darin is putting tape on the floor while Abel holds the measuring tape to gauge the distance. "How big should this first part be?" asks Darin.

Sabrina looks at the scrap paper and says, "Don't make it bigger than 120 centimeters, or else it will be too big for the screen. What about maybe 100 across and then 50 or 60 down?"

Abel measures 100 centimeters as Darin adheres tape of the same length. Then, Abel measures 50 centimeters, perpendicular to the first strip of tape, and Darin puts down the second strip of tape. Meanwhile, Shanna draws the lines on the Sphero.edu screen (see Figure 6.2). She suggests, "We could just let the lines get ten centimeters smaller each time the path turns. That way it's easy to draw on the screen because ten centimeters is just one square." The group agrees, and proceeds to create their taped path as Shanna draws the path on the Chromebook. The group tests their path and finds that Sphero stays on the tape for the most part. On their worksheets, the students attribute the deviations to a path drawing with lines that were not completely straight.

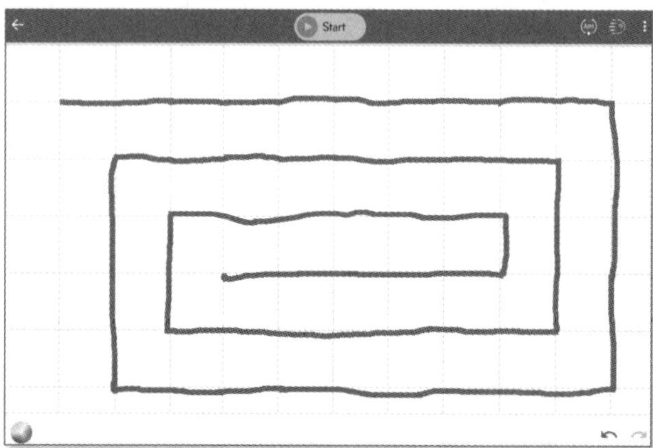

Figure 6.2 Sabrina, Abel, Darin, and Shanna's Sphero path.

Meanwhile, Lupe, Corina, Cherie, and Miriam work on their group's scale model. Although they are also able to determine that one grid square corresponds to ten centimeters of robot movement, they approach the tape path differently than the previous group. Instead of measuring as they place the tape, they begin by making a shaped path and drawing a similar shape on the Sphero.edu screen (as shown in Figure 6.3). When they test their path, they realize that although Sphero follows a similar shape, it does not follow the tape they placed on the floor. Instead, the robot's path is much smaller. Miriam wonders aloud, "It's the same shape, I don't get why it's not staying on the tape."

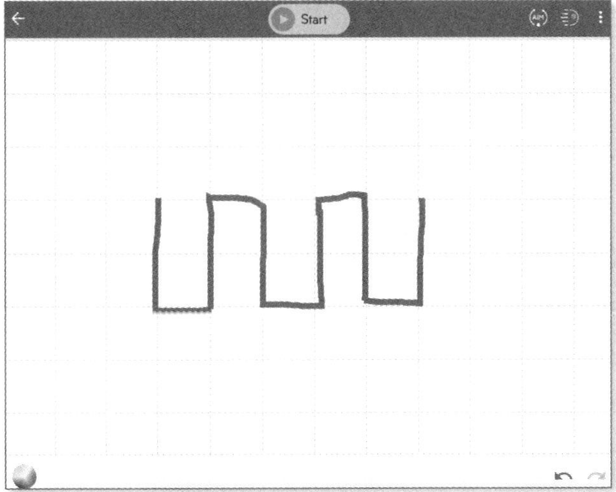

Figure 6.3 Lupe, Corina, Cherie, and Miriam's Sphero path.

"Maybe if we just make the drawing bigger, but the same shape? Like the pictures at the beginning of class?" asks Cherie.

Lupe suddenly realizes, "Because it's supposed to be a scale drawing, we probably need to use that ten centimeter equals one square."

Corina agrees. "We should measure the tape so we can figure out how many big it's supposed to be on the screen."

Lupe uses the tape measure to measure the tape lengths while Cherie records the measurements on scrap paper. Miriam and Corina discuss how to translate the tape measurements into screen measurements and create the revised path program shown in Figure 6.4. The group tests the new program, and are delighted to see Sphero follow the tape on the floor.

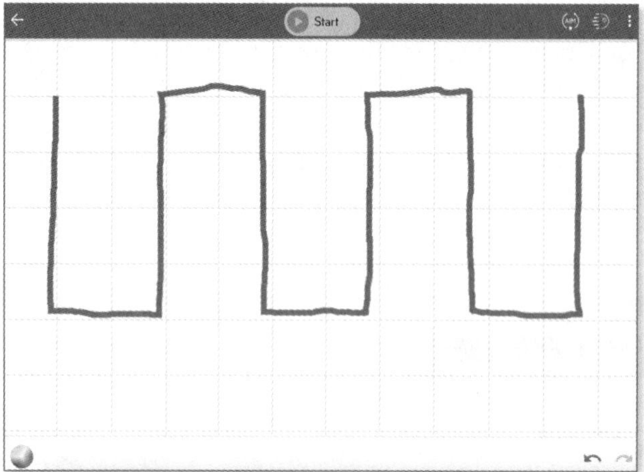

Figure 6.4   Lupe, Corina, Cherie, and Miriam's revised Sphero path.

As class time comes to an end, Mr. Smith asks students to wrap up their work, and to be sure they've drawn pictures of their paths on the worksheets so they can answer questions about scale drawings. Most of the students are reluctant to stop what they are doing, and Mr. Smith can see that they are engaged in interesting conversations related to scale drawings. He tells students they will get a chance to work with the robots again in this unit and asks everyone to finish their worksheets as homework. To close the lesson, he instructs them to return to the Learnzillion online lesson, and complete the Cool Down activity as an exit ticket to gauge their understanding of scale drawings. Tomorrow, he plans to start class with a discussion of some of the paths and draw upon the activity to introduce scale factor. He'll also invite some students to show their programs to the rest of the class so they can discuss how they figured out path programs that would match the taped shapes.

Overall, Mr. Smith feels like this lesson was a success. The students clearly enjoyed working with the robots, and their group conversations were rich with mathematical language and problem solving. Some students will need additional support, as he can see they are still struggling to make sense of scale drawings. Because this is the first lesson of the unit, they will spend several more lessons developing ideas about scale. Nevertheless, he was able to introduce scale drawings in a way that engaged all students, and provide a common experience to refer back to throughout the unit. Mr. Smith looks forward to tomorrow's class discussion, and to sharing the lesson success with the technology coordinator.

Reflection Questions

Now, consider Mr. Smith's use of technology in this lesson. As you reflect and discuss with colleagues, consider what happened in Mr. Smith's lesson and how it compares with Ms. Atwood's class.

- Would you consider this a technology-rich lesson? Why or why not?

- What was the purpose of Mr. Smith's technology use in this lesson?

- How did Mr. Smith's integration of technology advance the teaching and learning of this math lesson?

- What were he and/or the students able to do with technology that was different from or better than what could have been done without technology?

- Were there any downsides to Mr. Smith's incorporation of technology in this lesson?

Next, consider the mathematical teaching practices in Mr. Smith's lesson, and how they compare with the practices in the first case.

- What were Mr. Smith's goals for this math lesson?

- Would you say that this lesson exemplifies what it means to teach and learn math through technology? Why or why not?

- To what extent did students have equitable access to learn and demonstrate their understanding in this lesson?

- Overall, what strengths do you see in this lesson? What opportunities do you notice?

What Does the Research Say?

The following research supports the use of technology as an educational tool:

- Across the multiple conceptions of 21st century skills, there has been a common thread of digital literacy and facility with digital age tools (Dede, 2010). A framework from the North Central Regional Educational Laboratory & Metiri Group (2003) identified digital age literacy as one of four essential 21st century skills. The Organization for Economic Co-operation and Development more broadly referred to competency with using tools interactively (2005). The Partnership for 21st Century Skills (2006) specified the need for students to develop ICT literacy. One of the four components of their 2019 Framework for 21st Century Learning is Information, Media, and Technology Skills, which require particular kinds of literacies in the digital age (Battelle for Kids). The most recent ISTE Standards provide a framework for stakeholders in education to support digital age learning. The growing emphasis on preparing students to use and learn with digital technologies highlights their importance with K–12 education.

- There is a growing body of research that shows the benefits of and potential for innovative tools in K–12 classrooms. Because of the variety of tools and scattershot way in which they are often implemented in schools, we look to small- and larger-scale studies involving technologies that are less typical in K–12 classrooms. In studies where educators have experimented with tools such as robotics, drones, virtual and augmented reality, and GPS devices, results have suggested increases in student interest in STEM, willingness to engage in classroom activities, and positive perceptions toward the content they are learning. Although further research is needed regarding teaching and learning with new digital tools, existing studies paint an optimistic picture for their potential impact on teaching and learning.

- Along with the growing emphasis on digital tools, a focus on computational thinking in both research and practice has emerged. ISTE includes Computational Thinker as a category within their Standards for Students (2016) and offers a separate document entitled, Computational Thinking Competencies for Educators. The National Research Council has convened workshops to consider the role of computational thinking in K–12 education (2010, 2011) and how it should be incorporated in school curriculum. Since the advent of programming languages decades ago, researchers have advocated for computational thinking in K–12 education and studied cognition relating to computing in schools (e.g., Clements & Gullo, 1984; Klahr & Carver, 1988; Liao & Bright, 1991; Papert, 1980). New calls for computational thinking and computer science education have ushered in a new era of research and programs aimed at developing students' computational thinking within the K–12 school curriculum (e.g., Aho, 2012; Grover & Pea, 2013; Lye & Koh, 2014; Weintrop et al., 2016; Wing, 2006).

The following research addresses teaching and learning math with technology:

- Since its introduction in U.S. classrooms during the 1960s "new math" era, computer programming has frequently been incorporated into or associated with the school math curriculum. In the late 1960s, Seymour Papert and colleagues developed the Logo educational programming language. This approach to programming incorporated a turtle cursor and gained traction in elementary math classrooms during the 1980s. The treatment of variables, functions, algorithmic thinking, representations, feedback, and abstraction within computer programming align with important aspects of algebraic thinking. Studies involving students' use of computer programing for learning math have shown it to be a productive approach to developing mathematical understanding (e.g., Clements & Gullo, 1984; Clements & Sarama, 1993, 1997; Harel & Papert, 1990; Klahr & Carver, 1988; Noss, 1986; Sutherland, 1989). The more recent resurgence of computer science in the school curriculum creates new opportunities to implement and study programming as a tool for mathematical learning (Kalelioğlu, 2015).

- Programming is not the only way in which students can learn math through technology. A wide variety of digital tools have been implemented and studied for their potential to support and expand student learning of math. As new mathematical tools have emerged, so too have the possibilities for enhancing teaching and learning. When combined with effective pedagogy, teacher professional development, and school curriculum, tools such as computer algebra systems (e.g., Heid, 1988; Heid, Blume, Hollebrands, & Piez, 2002), calculators (e.g., Doerr & Zangor, 2000; Penglase & Arnold, 1996), data analysis tools and software (e.g., Lee & Hollebrands, 2011), dynamic geometry environments (e.g., Laborde, 2000; Zbiek & Hollebrands, 2008), and other software (e.g., Lantz-Anderson, Linderoth, & Säljö, 2009; Roschelle et al., 2010) have positively impacted how and what math is learned in schools.

Reflecting on Technology in Math Teaching

Reading the cases of Ms. Atwood and Mr. Smith's seventh-grade classrooms, you probably noticed big differences in how the math was taught, and how technology was used to support their math teaching. In Ms. Atwood's class, she taught a shorter lesson so students would have a chance to play with the coding robots.

While she pointed out a potential connection between the math lesson and the robot activity, students could play with the robots without explicitly attending to ideas about scale drawings. Mr. Smith was also enthusiastic about incorporating coding robots in his classroom, but he designed an activity where students deepened their understanding of scaled drawings by using the robots to create scaled paths. The teachers in both cases emphasized similar math content and used the same kinds of technologies (interactive whiteboards, Chromebooks, and coding robots). Both were technology-rich lessons, but Mr. Smith used the robots in a way that helped students learn about math and technology. In both situations, students worked in groups and seemed to have equitable opportunities to interact with the technology. In Mr. Smith's class, the math tasks students completed with technology were differentiated according to students' performance on a pre-assessment, thereby tailoring the experiences more to students' individualized needs. At the end of each lesson, Ms. Atwood and Mr. Smith were pleased with students' engagement and eager to find more class time for students to work with these new digital tools. Table 6.1 compares the cases of Ms. Atwood and Mr. Smith.

TABLE 6.1 Use of Technology in the Cases of Ms. Atwood and Mr. Smith

	The Case of Ms. Atwood	The Case of Mr. Smith
What technology is used?	Interactive whiteboard, shared Chromebooks, coding robots	Interactive whiteboard, shared Chromebooks, Sphero robots
What math is emphasized?	Compute lengths from a scale drawing, and reproduce a scale drawing at a different scale.	Compute lengths from a scale drawing, and reproduce a scale drawing at a different scale.
How is the lesson launched?	Ms. Atwood displays curriculum materials on the interactive whiteboard, and students participate OR there is a guessing activity about enlargements and reductions.	Mr. Smith launches the lesson with online curriculum materials to introduce concepts relating to scale drawings.
Who is doing the math in this lesson?	Students apply what they see and hear at the beginning of the lesson to complete exercises about scale drawings.	Students work in groups to find a scale factor, and create scaled paths for robots to follow. They record their thinking individually on worksheets.
When and how is technology used in the lesson?	An interactive whiteboard is used to display curriculum materials and examples about scale drawings. Chromebooks are used to explore making paths for coding robots.	An interactive whiteboard is used to display an online lesson about scale drawings. Students follow along on Chromebooks that are later used to make scaled paths for coding robots.

One way of thinking about the contrast between Ms. Atwood and Mr. Smith's technology use in these lessons is to ask: *"Are students learning how to use technology during math, or are they learning math through using technology?"* Ms. Atwood saw some connections between her math lesson and the coding robots she was eager to use in her classroom, but the learning activity did not emphasize those potential connections. On the other hand, Mr. Smith designed an activity that enabled students to learn about both math and coding robots in tandem.

Equitable access to technology and math is an important consideration in any lesson. In both classrooms, multiple students participated in the beginning of the lesson, and all students had access to work with the coding robots in small collaborative groups. Mr. Smith also planned to meet student needs by administering a pre-assessment and designing an open-ended task that would be appropriately challenging for all students. The technology-rich tasks, combined with norms for classroom discussion in his classroom, sparked rich mathematical conversations and learning opportunities for all students.

Recommendations for Practice

Ms. Atwood and Mr. Smith's lessons provide an example of what it could look like if: *Instead of using technology for its own sake, what if we use technology in the service of learning rich, interesting math?* But what can you do to transform your classroom to teach and learn through technology? Here are three suggestions to consider:

1. Play with new technologies that interest you so you can identify connections with your math curriculum.

Reach out to colleagues and coaches to learn more about technology! Both Ms. Atwood and Mr. Smith were inspired to use coding robots in their classrooms. Attending conferences and workshops in your community, or from national organizations such as ISTE or NCTM, can introduce you to new technologies you may never have considered for your classroom. If you do attend a conference, check out exhibitors' booths for new ideas, and try to attend at least one session about a technology you've never tried before. You can also read about new educational technologies in books and teacher journals such as *Empowered Learner* and *Mathematics Teacher: Learning and Teaching in PK–12.* Of course, there is a wealth of resources available online as well where you can learn about cutting-edge technologies that may pique your interest.

Maybe you heard a plug about a new digital tool or discovered something you would like to know more about for your classroom. Colleagues are another great resource. If you have a technology coach or coordinator, like Mr. Smith did, you could reach out to her/him to learn more. Even if you don't know of anyone you can reach out to, online networks of educators provide a supportive community through blogs and social media platforms. However you choose to connect, staying abreast of educational technology innovations will expand your horizons for what technologies are available to incorporate into your teaching. Explore and play with new technologies when you get the chance so you can identify opportunities to support your teaching and your students' learning. This does not necessarily mean you have to be an expert before you try out new technologies with your students. You can often design instruction that lets you learn about technology with and from your students!

2. Design technology-rich instructional activities that give students a chance to develop technological literacy at the same time they are exploring interesting math.

Once you have identified an interesting tool and have had a chance to familiarize yourself with it, the next step is to connect the tool with your teaching and learning goals. Unless you have instructional time available for learning *about* technology, you will likely need to figure out how you can design instructional activities that enable students to learn **with** technology. Some educational technologies have their own curriculum materials available. Even if this is the case, and you determine that the materials align with your teaching and learning needs, you must still determine how to incorporate outside resources into your math curriculum. Also ask yourself what students will need to learn in order to use the technology itself. Ideally, digital tools will be intuitive and user-friendly enough to require minimum training for student use. If not, you'll have to make some judgment calls about how much class time is worth investing in a tool. This is often informed by how frequently and extensively you plan to use the tool.

As you design technology-rich instructional activities, some questions you might consider include:

- How familiar are students with the technologies we'll be using? How much will I need to teach about the technology before we can learn with the technology?

- Is the technology helping students learn more about a mathematical idea? (The mere presence of numbers or potential to connect with a math topic does not a math lesson make.)

- Does the activity help students make math connections? (Do not simply assume that students will pick up on nuanced math connections, or transfer their technology experiences to their math learning. Build those opportunities into the activity and lesson.)

3. When possible, give students a chance to learn with cutting edge technologies through purposeful play.

If students are excited to work with a new and novel technology, there is a good chance they will want to dive in and explore. Lengthy tutorials or step-by-step technology-use experiences can lose students' interest quickly, and before you know it, a number of students have gotten sidetracked or lost. For this reason, you may want to minimize more structured tutorials and instead spend time establishing some baseline competencies and ground rules. Then, design instruction so that students can explore and learn through purposeful play. These experiences are often collaborative (which fits well in situations where technology device access is limited). Providing self-paced learning activities or open-ended problems that students can solve in a variety of ways gives students a chance to learn about math and technology through means that are more responsive to individual student needs.

Connecting Cases with Standards

In this chapter, the cases of Ms. Atwood and Mr. Smith demonstrate ways that technology can be used to teach a seventh-grade geometry lesson. Following, you will find Common Core State Standards for Mathematics and ISTE Standards for Students and for Educators that align, to some extent, with one or both of the cases in this chapter. It may be useful for you to discuss and consider with colleagues how the case aligns with math standards in your state or district, as well as ISTE Standards for Administrators and for Coaches.

Math Content Standard

CCSS.MATH.CONTENT.7.G.A.1. Solve problems involving scale drawings of geometric figures, including computing actual lengths and areas from a scale drawing and reproducing a scale drawing at a different scale.

Mathematical Practice Standards

- Make sense of problems and persevere in solving them

- Reason abstractly and quantitatively

- Model with mathematics

- Use appropriate tools strategically

- Attend to precision

ISTE Standards for Educators

1b. Pursue professional interests by creating and actively participating in local and global learning networks.

2c. Model for colleagues the identification, exploration, evaluation, curation and adoption of new digital resources and tools for learning.

4a. Dedicate planning time to collaborate with colleagues to create authentic learning experiences that leverage technology.

5b. Design authentic learning activities that align with content area standards and use digital tools and resources to maximize active, deep learning.

6a. Foster a culture where students take ownership of their learning goals and outcomes in both independent and group settings.

6c. Create learning opportunities that challenge students to use a design process and computational thinking to innovate and solve problems.

7a. Provide alternative ways for students to demonstrate competency and reflect on their learning using technology.

ISTE Standards for Students

1d. Students understand the fundamental concepts of technology operations, demonstrate the ability to choose, use and troubleshoot current technologies and are able to transfer their knowledge to explore emerging technologies.

4b. Students select and use digital tools to plan and manage a design process that considers design constraints and calculated risks.

4d. Students exhibit a tolerance for ambiguity, perseverance and the capacity to work with open-ended problems.

5a. Students formulate problem definitions suited for technology-assisted methods such as data analysis, abstract models and algorithmic thinking in exploring and finding solutions.

5c. Students break problems into component parts, extract key information, and develop descriptive models to understand complex systems or facilitate problem-solving.

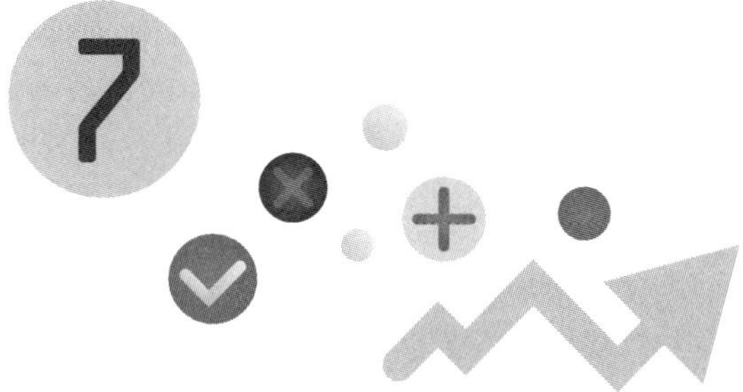

A TOOL FOR INTEGRATING TECHNOLOGY IN YOUR MATH CLASSROOM

Technology-rich math lessons require teachers to consider at least two dimensions: technology integration and math teaching practices.

THE GOAL THROUGHOUT THIS BOOK has been to bridge research and practice about educational technology and math teaching and learning. Chapters two through six include a total of ten different classroom cases ranging from Grade six through more advanced high school math content. In each chapter, the paired cases highlighted technology use for common math goals, but the ways in which technology combined with effective teaching practices differed. Whereas the first case in each chapter highlighted common, well-intentioned uses of technology in secondary math classrooms, the second case provided a vision for what more transformative technology use might look like when combined with best practices for teaching math.

Table 7.1 summarizes the grade levels, math content, and technology availability in these classroom cases. As you have read, the previous chapters include a variety of mathematical topics and technology availability scenarios. Classroom cases illustrate that effective math teaching with technology does not necessarily require having more technology, but rather leveraging available technologies in effective ways. Students do not need 1:1 laptops or tablets in order for math teachers to integrate technology into math lessons. Conversely, having technology in the classroom does not necessarily mean that its use positively impacts the teaching and learning of math.

TABLE 7.1 Grade Level, Math Content, and Technology Availability in Cases

Chapter and Grade Level	Teacher	Math Content	Technology Availability
Chapter Two: Grade Eight	Ms. Parks	Multiplying binomials	Shared classroom computers
	Mr. Chavez		Shared student laptops
Chapter Three: Grade Nine	Ms. King	Algebra I: Solving equations using multiple representations	1:1 student laptops
	Mr. Lennon		Paired student laptops
Chapter Four: Grade 10	Mr. Simone	Geometry: Trigonometric ratios	Teacher iPad; Shared classroom computers
	Ms. Davis		Teacher computer; Shared student iPads
Chapter Five: Grade Six	Ms. Keys	Statistics and Data: Box plots	Bring-your-own-device (BYOD) or shared classroom tablets
	Ms. Young		BYOD or shared classroom tablets
Chapter Six: Grade Seven	Ms. Atwood	Geometry and Measurement: Scale Drawings	Shared student Chromebooks
	Mr. Smith		Shared student Chromebooks

Technology-rich math lessons require teachers to consider at least two dimensions: technology integration and math teaching practices. An impactful tool for supporting teachers with evaluating and selecting technology emerged from research with a colleague (Thomas & Edson, 2017). The Digital Instructional Material Framework combines technology integration and effective math teaching practices in a matrix. Within this framework, we consider three levels of technology integration: replacement, amplification, and transformation (Hughes, Thomas, & Scharber, 2006). Replacement refers to technology integration that replaces non-tech resources but with little value added. Amplification integration results in a noticeable enhancement. Transformation enables experiences that would not be possible without technology. The second dimension identifies what is to be replaced, amplified, or transformed through technology integration. We highlight the eight effective math teaching practices as defined by NCTM (2014).

The resulting framework (Table 7.2) is a matrix that teachers or stakeholders can use to evaluate or plan for technology-rich math instruction. If you think back to some of the cases highlighted in this book, you might find it more difficult to place the first cases in each chapter on this framework, as compared with the second cases. For example, in Chapter seven, Ms. Atwood used coding robots in her lesson about scale drawings, but can you identify any teaching practices that were replaced, amplified, or transformed through her use of the robots? Mr. Smith also used coding robots for similar purposes, but you might say that the robots amplified or transformed how he *implemented tasks that promoted reasoning and problem solving,* or amplified *using and connecting mathematical representations.*

TABLE 7.2 Digital Instructional Material Framework

	Replacement	Amplification	Transformation
Establish mathematical goals to focus learning.			
Implement tasks that promote reasoning and problem solving.			
Use and connect mathematical representations.			
Facilitate meaningful mathematical discourse.			
Pose purposeful questions.			
Build procedural fluency from conceptual understanding.			
Support productive struggle in learning mathematics.			
Elicit and use evidence of student thinking.			

The Digital Instructional Material Framework is a tool you can use in your classroom or school to help identify or evaluate the impact of technology integration on your math teaching practices. If you are more familiar with the Substitution-Augmentation-Modification-Redefinition (SAMR) model, you might think about four columns of technology integration rather than the three listed in the matrix. Likewise, if you integrate technology into a science, social studies, or reading class, look to standards and professional organizations to identify teaching practices outside of math.

In addition to the dimensions shown in the Digital Instructional Material Framework, teachers and stakeholders must consider a number of overarching concerns including equity and access, and incorporating technology with existing curriculum. Each chapter specifically attends to equity and access, highlighting ways in which technology and teaching practices can meet individual student needs. Technology can be a tool that allows students more access to interesting math, or it can function as a reward, or gatekeeper, that denies access to some students. If technology is truly used as a learning tool, then it must be integrated in ways that alleviate, not exacerbate, inequities among students.

Integrating technology into existing math curriculum is another practical challenge, especially when math textbook implementation expectations are high. Some curricula include technology components, but it is up to teachers and administrators to determine the value added by those resources. This book identifies a number of potentially valuable resources and ways to use them, but the digital age has placed new burdens on teachers to act as curators of the vast wealth of digital resources available online. Determining how and which resources fit with adopted curriculum materials requires professional knowledge and discretion. It is the author's sincere hope that this book contributes to your purposeful selection and implementation of digital resources for effectively teaching math in the future.

REFERENCES

Aho, A. V. (2012). Computation and computational thinking. *Computer Journal, 55,* 832-835.

Akçayır, M., & Akçayır, G. (2017). Advantages and challenges associated with augmented reality for education: A systematic review of the literature. *Educational Research Review, 20,* 1-11.

An, S., & Wu, Z. (2012). Enhancing mathematics teachers' knowledge of students' thinking from assessing and analyzing misconceptions in homework. *International Journal of Science and Mathematics Education, 10,* 717-753.

Atkinson, C. (1942). Radio in the classroom: Best current practices and theories. *The Clearing House, 16*(5), 291-293.

Baroody, A. J., Purpura, D. J., Eiland, M. D., Reid, E. E., & Paliwal, V. (2016). Does fostering reasoning strategies for relatively difficult basic combinations promote transfer by K–3 students? *Journal of Educational Psychology, 108*(4), 576-591.

Batelle for Kids. (2019). *Framework for 21st Century Learning.* Partnership for 21st Century Learning. Retrieved from http://www.battelleforkids.org/networks/ p21/frameworks-resources

Beatty, R., & Geiger, V. (2009). Technology, communication, and collaboration: Re-thinking communities of inquiry, learning, and practice. In C. Hoyles, J.B. Lagrange (Eds.) *Mathematics Education and Technology-Rethinking the Terrain* (pp. 251-284). Boston, MA: Springer.

Berry, R. Q. III, & Ellis, M. W. (2013). Multidimensional teaching. *Mathematics Teaching in the Middle School, 19*(3), 172-178.

Black, P., & Wiliam, D. (1998a). Inside the black box: Raising standards through classroom assessment. *Phi Delta Kappan, 80*(1), 139-48.

Black, P., & Wiliam, D. (1998b). Assessment and classroom learning. *Assessment in Education, 5*(1), 7-74.

Boaler, J. (2015). Fluency without fear: Research evidence on the best ways to learn math facts. Retrieved from https://www.youcubed.org/evidence/ fluency-without-fear/

Borba, M. C., Askar, P., Engelbrecht, J., Gadanidis, G., Llinares, S., & Aguilar, M. S. (2016). Blended learning, e-learning and mobile learning in mathematics education. *ZDM, 48*(5), 589-610.

Bray, W. S. (2013). How to leverage the potential of mathematical errors. *Teaching Children Mathematics, 19*(7), 424-431.

Burger, W. B., & Shaughnessy, J. M. (1986). Characterizing the van Hiele levels of development in geometry. *Journal for Research in Mathematics Education, 17*(1), 31-48.

Carnahan, C., Crowley, K., Hummel, L., & Sheehy, L. (2016, March). New perspectives on education: Drones in the classroom. In *Society for Information Technology & Teacher Education International Conference* (pp. 1920-1924). Association for the Advancement of Computing in Education (AACE).

Chapin, S. H., O'Connor, C., & Anderson, N. C. (2013). *Talk moves: A teacher's guide for using classroom discussions in math, Grades K–6*. Sausalito, CA: Math Solutions.

Clements, D. H. & Gullo, D. F. (1984). Effects of computer programming on young children's cognitions. *Journal of Educational Psychology, 76,* 1051-1058.

Clements, D. H. & Sarama, J. (1993). Research on Logo: Effects and efficacy. *Journal of Computing in Childhood Education, 3-4,* 263-290.

Clements, D. H. & Sarama, J. (1997). Computers support algebraic thinking. *Teaching Children Mathematics, 3,* 320-325.

Clements, D. H., & Sarama, J. (2009). *Learning and teaching early math: The learning trajectories approach.* New York, NY: Routledge.

Choppin, J. (2011). The impact of professional noticing on teachers' adaptations of challenging tasks. *Mathematical Thinking and Learning, 13*(3), 175-197.

Cobb, P. (1994). Where is the mind? Constructivist and sociocultural perspectives on mathematical development. *Educational Researcher, 23*(7), 13-20.

Cross, D. I., Hudson, R. A., Adefope, O., Lee, M. Y., Rapacki, L, & Perez, A. (2012). Success made probable: African-American girls' exploration in statistics through project-based learning. *Journal of Urban Mathematics Education, 5*(2), 55-86.

Darling-Hammond, L. (2010). Teacher education and the American future. *Journal of Teacher Education, 61*(1-2), 35-47.

Davis, J., & Martin, D. B. (2018). 2008—Racism, assessment, and instructional practices: Implications for mathematics teachers of African American students. *Journal of Urban Mathematics Education, 11*(1-2).

Dede, C. (2010). Comparing frameworks for 21st century skills. 21st century skills: *Rethinking how students learn, 20,* 51-76.

Dewey, J. (1902). **The child and the curriculum.** Chicago, IL: The University of Chicago Press.

Dishon, G. (2017). New data, old tensions: Big data, personalized learning, and the challenges of progressive education. **Theory and Research in Education,** *15*(3), 272-289.

Doerr, H. M., & Zangor, R. (2000). Creating meaning for and with the graphing calculator. **Educational Studies in Mathematics,** *41*(2), 143-163.

Eguchi, A. (2014, July). Robotics as a learning tool for educational transformation. In **Proceeding of 4th international workshop teaching robotics, teaching with robotics & 5th international conference robotics in education, Padova (Italy)** (pp. 27-34).

Erlwanger, S. H. (1973). Benny's conception of rules and answers in IPI mathematics. **Journal of Children's Mathematical Behavior,** *1,* 7-26.

Eureka Math. (2015). Lesson 16: Relating scale drawings to ratios and rates. Retrieved from https://www.engageny.org/resource/ grade-7-mathematics-module-1-topic-d-lesson-16

Faber, J. M., Luyten, H., & Visscher, A. J. (2017). The effects of a digital formative assessment tool on mathematics achievement and student motivation: Results of a randomized experiment. **Computers & Education,** *106,* 83-96.

Fehr, H. F., & Fey, J. (1969). The secondary school mathematics curriculum improvement study. **The American Mathematical Monthly,** *76*(10), 1132-1137.

Ferrini-Mundy, J., & Martin, W. G. (2000). **Principles and standards for school mathematics.** Reston, VA: National Council of Teachers of Mathematics (NCTM).

Franke, M., Webb, N., Chan, A., Battey, D., Ing, M., Freund, D., & De, T. (2009). Eliciting student thinking in elementary mathematics classrooms: Practices that support understanding. *Journal of Teacher Education, 60,* 380-392.

Franklin, C., Kader, G., Mewborn, D., Moreno, J., Peck, R., Perry, M., & Schaeffer, R. (2005). *Guidelines for assessment and instruction in statistics education (GAISE) report: A Pre-K–12 curriculum framework.* Alexandria, VA: American Statistical Association.

Fuson, K. C., & Murata, A. (2007). Integrating NRC principles and the NCTM Process Standards to form a class learning path model that individualizes within whole-class activities. *National Council of Supervisors of Mathematics Journal of Mathematics Education Leadership, 10*(1), 72-91.

Galbraith, P. & Haines, C. (1998). Disentangling the nexus: Attitudes to mathematics and technology in a computer learning environment. *Educational Studies in Mathematics, 35*(3), 275-290.

Geist, E. (2010). The anti-anxiety curriculum: Combating math anxiety in the classroom. *Journal of Instructional Psychology, 37*(1), 24-31.

Gobert, J. D., Sao Pedro, M. A., Baker, R. S., Toto, E., & Montalvo, O. (2012). Leveraging educational data mining for real-time performance assessment of scientific inquiry skills within microworlds. *Journal of Educational Data Mining, 4*(1), 111-143.

Gohl, E. M., Gohl, D., & Wolf, M. A. (2009). Assessments and technology: A powerful combination for improving teaching and learning. In L.M. Pinkus (Ed.) *Meaningful measurement: The role of assessments in improving high school education in the twenty-first century* (pp. 183-197). Washington, DC: Alliance for Excellent Education.

Goos, M., Galbraith, P., Renshaw, P., & Geiger, V. (2000). Reshaping teacher and student roles in technology-enriched classrooms. *Mathematics Education Research Journal, 12*(3), 303-320.

Granito, M. & Chernobilsky, E. (2012). The effect of technology on a student's motivation and knowledge retention. *Northeastern Educational Research Association Proceedings 2012.*

Grover, S., & Pea, R. (2013). Computational thinking in K–12: A review of the state of the field. *Educational Researcher, 42*(1), 38-43.

Gutstein, E., & Peterson, B. (2013). Introduction. In E. Gutstein & B. Peterson (Eds.), *Rethinking mathematics: Teaching social justice by the numbers, 2nd ed* (pp. xi-xiii). Milwaukee, WI: Rethinking Schools.

Harel, I., & Papert, S. (1990). Software design as a learning environment. *Interactive Learning Environments, 1,* 1-32.

Hattie, J. A. C. (2009). *Visible learning: A synthesis of over 800 meta-analyses relating to achievement.* New York, NY: Routledge.

Heid, M. K. (1988). Re-sequencing skills and concepts in applied calculus using the computer as a tool. *Journal for Research in Mathematics Education, 19*(1), 3-25.

Heid, M. K., Blume, G., Hollebrands, K., & Piez, C. (2002). Implications from research on the use of CAS in the teaching and learning of mathematics. *Mathematics Teacher, 95*(8), 586-591.

Hoadley, C. M., Hsi, S., & Berman, B. P. (1995). The Multimedia Forum Kiosk and SpeakEasy, *Proceedings of ACM Multimedia.* New York, NY: ACM Press.

Hsi, S., & Hoadley, C. M. (1997). Productive discussions in science: Gender equity through electronic discourse. *Journal of Science Education and Technology, 6,* 23-36.

Hughes, J., Thomas, R., & Scharber, C. (2006). Assessing technology integration: The RAT—replacement, amplification, and transformation—framework. In C. Crawford, R. Carlsen, K. McFerrin, J. Price, R. Weber, & D. Willis (Eds.), *Proceedings of SITE 2006-Society for Information Technology & Teacher Education international conference* (pp. 1616-1620). Orlando, FL: Association for the Advancement of Computing in Education.

Hurme, T., & Jarvela, S. (2005). Students' activity in computer-supportive collaborative problem solving in mathematics. *International Journal of Computers for Mathematical Learning, 10,* 49-73.

Illustrative Mathematics and Learnzillion. (2019). Lesson 1: What are scaled copies? Retrieved from https://learnzillion.com/lesson_plans/28457-lesson-1-what-are-scaled-copies/

International Society for Technology in Education. (1998). *National educational technology standards for students.* ISTE.

International Society for Technology in Education. (2000). *National educational technology standards for students: Connecting curriculum and technology.* ISTE.

International Society for Technology in Education. (2001). *Technology standards for school administrators (TSSA).* ISTE.

Irving, K. E. (2006). The impact of educational technology on student achievement: Assessment. *Science Educator, 15*(1), 13-20.

Jacobs, V. R., Lamb, L. L., & Philipp, R. A. (2010). Professional noticing of children's mathematical thinking. *Journal for Research in Mathematics Education, 41*(2), 169-202.

Kalelioğlu, F. (2015). A new way of teaching programming skills to K–12 students: Code.org. *Computers in Human Behavior, 52,* 200-210.

Kamii, C., & Dominick, A. (1998). The harmful effects of algorithms in grades 1-4. In L. Morrow & M. Kenney (Eds.), *The teaching and learning of algorithms in school mathematics* (pp. 130-139). Reston, VA: NCTM.

Kebritchi, M., Hirumi, A., & Bai, H. (2010). The effects of modern mathematics computer games on mathematics achievement and class motivation. *Computers & Education, 55*(2), 427-443.

Kisker, E. E., Lipka, J., Adams, B. L., Rickard, A., Andrew-Ihrke, D., Yanez, E. E., & Millard, A. (2012). The potential of a culturally based supplemental mathematics curriculum to improve the mathematics performance of Alaska native and other students. *Journal for Research in Mathematics Education, 43*(1), 75-113.

Klahr, D., & Carver, S. M. (1988). Cognitive objectives in a LOGO debugging curriculum: Instruction, learning, and transfer. *Cognitive Psychology, 20,* 362-404.

Laborde, C. (2000). Dynamic geometry environments as a source of rich learning contexts for the complex activity of proving. *Educational Studies in Mathematics, 44*(1-2), 151-161.

Lantz-Anderson, A., Linderoth, J., & Säljö, R. (2009). What's the problem? Meaning making and learning to do mathematical word problems in the context of digital tools. *Instructional Science, 37*(4), 325-343.

Larson, M. (2017). Breaking barriers: Actionable approaches to reach each and every learner in mathematics. Presented at Innov8 Conference, National Council of Teachers of Mathematics, Las Vegas, NV.

Leahy, S., Lyon, C., Thompson, M., & Wiliam, D. (2005). Classroom assessment: Minute by minute, day by day. *Educational Leadership, 63*(3), 18-24.

Lee, H. S., & Hollebrands, K. F. (2011). Characterizing and developing teachers' knowledge for teaching statistics with technology. In C. Batanero, G. Burrill, & C. Reading (Eds.), *Teaching statistics in school mathematics — Challenges for teaching and teacher education: A joint ICMI/IASE study* (pp. 359-369). New York, NY: Springer.

Lesh, R., Post, T., & Behr, M. (1987). Representations and translations among representations in mathematics learning and problem solving. In C. Janvier (Ed.) *Problems of representation in the teaching and learning of mathematics* (pp. 33-40). Hillsdale, NJ: Erlbaum.

Li, Q., & Ma, X. (2010). A meta-analysis of the effects of computer technology on school students' mathematical learning. *Educational Psychology Review, 22*(3), 215-243.

Liao, Y-K. C. & Bright, G. W. (1991). Effects of computer programming on cognitive outcomes: A meta-analysis. *Journal of Educational Computing Research, 7*(3), 251-268.

Lindvall, C. M. & Cox, R. C. (1970). The IPI evaluation program. *AERA Monograph Series on Curriculum Evaluation, No. 5*. Chicago, IL: Rand McNally and Company.

Lye, S. Y., & Koh, J. H. L. (2014). Review on teaching and learning of computational thinking through programming: What is next for K–12?. *Computers in Human Behavior, 41*, 51-61.

Macfadyen, L. P., Dawson, S., Pardo, A., & Gaševic, D. (2014). Embracing big data in complex educational systems: The learning analytics imperative and the policy challenge. *Research & Practice in Assessment, 9*, 17-28.

Merchant, Z., Goetz, E. T., Cifuentes, L., Keeney-Kennicutt, W., & Davis, T. J. (2014). Effectiveness of virtual reality-based instruction on students' learning outcomes in K–12 and higher education: A meta-analysis. *Computers & Education, 70*, 29-40.

Middleton, J. A., & Spanias, P. A. (1999). Motivation for achievement in mathematics: Findings, generalizations, and criticisms of the research. *Journal for Research in Mathematics Education, 30*(1), 65-88.

Mistler-Jackson, M., & Songer, N. B. (2000). Student motivation and internet technology: Are students empowered to learn science? *Journal of Research in Science Teaching, 37*(5), 459-479.

Moreno-Armella, L., Hegedus, S., & Kaput, J. (2008). From static to dynamic mathematics: Historical and representational perspectives. *Educational Studies in Mathematics, 68,* 99-111.

Moschkovich, J. N. (1999). Understanding the needs of Latino students in reform-oriented mathematics classrooms. In L.Ortiz-Franco, N. G. Hernández, & Y. de la Cruz (Eds.), *Changing the faces of mathematics: Perspectives on Latinos* (pp. 5-12). Reston, VA: NCTM.

Moschkovich, J. (2007). Examining mathematical discourse practices. *For the Learning of Mathematics, 27*(1), 24-30.

Moschkovich, J. N. (2011). Supporting mathematical reasoning and sense making for English learners. In M.E. Strutchens & J. R. Quander (Eds.), *Focus in high school mathematics: Fostering reasoning and sense making for all students* (pp. 17-36). Reston, VA: NCTM.

Moyer, P. S. (2001). Are we having fun yet? How teachers use manipulatives to teach mathematics. *Educational Studies in Mathematics, 47*(2), 175-197.

National Council of Teachers of Mathematics. Commission on Standards for School Mathematics. (1989). *Curriculum and evaluation standards for school mathematics.* Reston, VA: Authors.

National Council of Teachers of Mathematics. (2006). *Curriculum focal points for prekindergarten through grade 8 mathematics: A quest for coherence.* Reston, VA: NCTM.

National Council of Teachers of Mathematics. (2014). *Principles to actions: Ensuring mathematical success for all.* Reston, VA: Authors.

National Mathematics Advisory Panel (NMAP). (2008). *Foundations for success: The final report of the National Mathematics Advisory Panel.* Washington, DC: U.S. Department of Education.

National Research Council. (2001a). *Adding it up: Helping children learn mathematics.* J. Kilpatrick, J. Swafford, and B. Findell (Eds.). Mathematics Learning Study Committee, Center for Education, Division of Behavioral and Social Studies and Education. Washington, DC: National Academies Press.

National Research Council. (2001b). *Knowing what students know: The science and design of educational assessment.* Washington, DC: National Academies Press.

National Research Council. (2010). *Committee for the workshops on computational thinking: Report of a workshop on the scope and nature of computational thinking.* Washington, DC: National Academies Press.

National Research Council. (2011). *Committee for the workshops on computational thinking: Report of a workshop on the scope and nature of computational thinking.* Washington, DC: National Academies Press.

North Central Regional Educational Laboratory & the Metiri Group. (2003). *enGauge 21st century skills: Literacy in the digital age.* Chicago, IL: North Central Regional Educational Laboratory.

Noss, R. (1986). Constructing a conceptual framework for elementary algebra through Logo programming. *Educational Studies in Mathematics, 17,* 335-357.

Nugent, G., Barker, B., Grandgenett, N., & Adamchuk, V. (2009, October). The use of digital manipulatives in K–12: robotics, GPS/GIS and programming. In *2009 39th IEEE Frontiers in Education Conference* (pp. 1-6). IEEE.

Olsher, S., Yerushalmy, M., & Chazan, D. (2016). How might the use of technology in formative assessment support changes in mathematics teaching? *For the Learning of Mathematics, 36*(3), 11-18.

Olson, L. (2003). Legal twists digital turns. *Education Week's Technology Counts, 22,* 11-16.

Organisation for Economic Co-operation and Development. (2005). *The definition and selection of key competencies: Executive summary.* Paris, France: OECD.

Papert, S. (1980). *Mindstorms: Children, computers, and powerful ideas.* New York, NY: Basic Books.

Partnership for 21st Century Skills. (2006). *A state leaders action guide to 21st century skills: A new vision for education.* Tuscon, AZ: Partnership for 21st Century Skills.

Pellegrino, J. W., & Quellmalz, E. S. (2010). Perspectives on the integration of technology and assessment. *Journal of Research on Technology in Education, 43*(2), 119-134.

Penglase, M., & Arnold, S. (1996). The graphics calculator in mathematics education: A critical review of recent research. *Mathematics Education Research Journal, 8*(1), 58-90.

Peters, H., Kruger, V., & Fitzpatrick, E. (2018). Creative digital technology ideas for the secondary school mathematics classroom. *Australian Mathematics Teacher, The, 74*(4), 3-8.

Piaget, J., & Duckworth, E. (1970). Genetic epistemology. *American Behavioral Scientist, 13*(3), 459-480.

Planas, N., & Civil, M. (2013). Language-as-resource and language-as-political: Tensions in the bilingual mathematics classroom. *Mathematics Education Research Journal, 25*(3), 361-378.

Popham, W. J. (2008). *Transformative assessment.* Alexandria, VA: Association for Supervision and Curriculum Development.

Riel, M. (1991). Learning circles: A functional analysis of educational telecomputing. *Interactive Learning Environments, 2,* 15-30.

Roschelle, J. M., Pea, R. D., Hoadley, C. M., Gordin, D. N., & Means, B. M. (2000). Changing how and what children learn in school with computer-based technologies. *Future of Children: Children and Computer Technology, 10*(2), 76-101.

Roschelle, J., Schechtman, N., Tatar, D., Hegedus, S., Hopkins, B., Empson, S., Knudson, J., & Gallagher, L. P. (2010). Integration of technology, curriculum, and professional development for advancing middle school mathematics: Three large-scale studies. *American Educational Research Journal, 47*(4), 833-78.

Scardamalia, M., & Bereiter, C. (1993). Technologies for knowledge-building discourse. *Communications of the ACM, 36,* 37-41.

Schifter, C., Natarajan, U., Ketelhut, D. J., & Kirschgessner, A. (2014). Data-driven decision-making: Facilitating teacher use of student data to inform classroom instruction. *Contemporary Issues in Technology and Teacher Education, 14*(4), 419-432.

Schifter, D. (2001). Learning to see the invisible: What skills and knowledge are needed to engage with students' mathematical ideas? In T. Wood, B.S. Nelson, & J. Warfield (Eds.), *Beyond classical pedagogy: Teaching elementary school mathematics,* (pp. 109-134). Mahwah, NJ: Erlbaum.

Schwendimann, B. A., Rodriguez-Triana, M. J., Vozniuk, A., Prieto, L. P., Boroujeni, M. S., Holzer, A., … & Dillenbourg, P. (2017). Perceiving learning at a glance: A systematic literature review of learning dashboard research. *IEEE Transactions on Learning Technologies, 10*(1), 30-41.

Sherin, M., Jacobs, V., & Philipp, R. (Eds.). (2011). *Mathematics teacher noticing: Seeing through teachers' eyes.* New York, NY: Routledge.

Sfard, A. (2001). There is more to discourse than meets the ears: Looking at thinking as communicating to learn more about mathematical learning. *Educational Studies in Mathematics, 46,* 13-57.

Smith, M. S., & Stein, M. K. (2011). *5 Practices for Orchestrating Productive Mathematics Discussions.* Reston, VA: NCTM.

Star, J. R., Chen, J. A., Taylor, M. W., Durkin, K., Dede, C., & Chao, T. (2014). Studying technology-based strategies for enhancing motivation in mathematics. *International Journal of STEM Education, 1-7.*

Sutherland, R. (1989). Providing a computer based framework for algebraic thinking. *Educational Studies in Mathematics, 20,* 317-344.

Suthers, D., Toth, E. E., & Weiner, A. (1997). An integrated approach to implementing collaborative inquiry in the classroom. *Proceedings of the Conference on Computer Supported Collaborative Learning.* Toronto, Ontario: CSCL.

Swan, M. (2001). Dealing with misconceptions in mathematics. In P. Gates (Ed.), *Issues in Mathematics Teaching* (pp. 147-165). New York, NY: Routledge.

Thomas, A. (2013). A study of Algebra 1 students' use of digital and print textbooks. (Doctoral dissertation, University of Missouri-Columbia. Columbia, MO.)

Thomas, A. (2017). Screencasting to support effective teaching practices. *Teaching Children Mathematics, 23*(8), 492-499.

Thomas, A., & Edson, A.J. (2017). A framework for mathematics teachers' evaluation of digital instructional materials: Integrating mathematics teaching practices with technology use in K–8 classrooms. In P. Resta & S. Smith (Eds.), *Proceedings of Society for Information Technology & Teacher Education international conference* (pp. 11-18). Austin, TX: Association for the Advancement of Computing in Education.

Torff, B., & Tirotta, R. (2010). Interactive whiteboards produce small gains in elementary students' self-reported motivation in mathematics. *Computers & Education, 54*(2), 37-383.

Tripathi, P. N. (2008). Developing mathematical understanding through multiple representations. *Mathematics Teaching in the Middle School, 13*(8), 438-445.

U.S. Department of Education, Office of Educational Technology. (2017). *Reimagining the role of technology in education: 2017 National Education Technology Plan update.* Washington, DC: Authors.

Vahey, P., Knudsen, J., Rafanan, K., & Lara-Meloy, T. (2012). Curricular activity systems supporting the use of dynamic representations to foster students' deep understanding of mathematics. In *Emerging technologies for the classroom* (pp. 15-30). New York, NY: Springer.

van Hiele, P. M. (1980). *Levels of thinking, how to meet them, how to avoid them.* Paper presented at the meeting of the National Council of Teachers of Mathematics, Seattle, WA.

Vygotsky, L. (1978). *Mind in society: The development of higher psychological processes.* Cambridge, MA: Harvard University Press.

Webb, M., Gibson, D., & Forkosh-Baruch, A. (2013). Challenges for information technology supporting educational assessment. *Journal of Computer Assisted Learning, 29*(5), 451-462.

Weintrop, D., Beheshti, E., Horn, M., Orton, K., Jona, K., Trouille, L., & Wilensky, U. (2016). Defining computational thinking for mathematics and science classrooms. *Journal of Science Education and Technology, 25*(1), 127-147.

White, T. (2006). Code talk: Student discourse and participation with networked handhelds. *International Journal of Computer-Supported Collaborative Learning, 1*(3), 359-382.

Wiliam, D. (2011). *Embedded Formative Assessment*. Bloomington, IN: Solution Tree Press.

Wing, J. (2006). Computational thinking. *Communications of the ACM, 49*(3), 33-36.

Xhakaj, F., Aleven, V., & McLaren, B. M. (2016). How teachers use data to help students learn: Contextual inquiry for the design of a dashboard. In *European Conference on Technology Enhanced Learning* (pp. 340-354). Springer, Cham.

Zbiek, R., & Hollebrands, K. (2008). A research-informed view of the process of incorporating mathematics technology into classroom practice by inservice and prospective teachers. In M. K. Heid & G. Blume (Eds.), *Research on technology in the learning and teaching of mathematics: Syntheses and perspectives*. Charlotte, NC: Information Age Publishers.

ISTE STANDARDS

ISTE Standards for Students

The ISTE Standards for Students emphasize the skills and qualities we want for students, enabling them to engage and thrive in a connected, digital world. The standards are designed for use by educators across the curriculum, with every age student, with a goal of cultivating these skills throughout a student's academic career.

1. Empowered Learner

Students leverage technology to take an active role in choosing, achieving and demonstrating competency in their learning goals, informed by the learning sciences. Students:

a. articulate and set personal learning goals, develop strategies leveraging technology to achieve them and reflect on the learning process itself to improve learning outcomes.

b. build networks and customize their learning environments in ways that support the learning process.

c. use technology to seek feedback that informs and improves their practice and to demonstrate their learning in a variety of ways.

d. understand the fundamental concepts of technology operations, demonstrate the ability to choose, use and troubleshoot current technologies and are able to transfer their knowledge to explore emerging technologies.

2. Digital Citizen

Students recognize the rights, responsibilities and opportunities of living, learning and working in an interconnected digital world, and they act and model in ways that are safe, legal and ethical. Students:

a. cultivate and manage their digital identity and reputation and are aware of the permanence of their actions in the digital world.

    b. engage in positive, safe, legal and ethical behavior when using technology, including social interactions online or when using networked devices.

    c. demonstrate an understanding of and respect for the rights and obligations of using and sharing intellectual property.

    d. manage their personal data to maintain digital privacy and security and are aware of data-collection technology used to track their navigation online.

3. Knowledge Constructor

Students critically curate a variety of resources using digital tools to construct knowledge, produce creative artifacts and make meaningful learning experiences for themselves and others. Students:

    a. plan and employ effective research strategies to locate information and other resources for their intellectual or creative pursuits.

    a. evaluate the accuracy, perspective, credibility and relevance of information, media, data or other resources.

    b. curate information from digital resources using a variety of tools and methods to create collections of artifacts that demonstrate meaningful connections or conclusions.

    c. build knowledge by actively exploring real-world issues and problems, developing ideas and theories and pursuing answers and solutions.

4. Innovative Designer

Students use a variety of technologies within a design process to identify and solve problems by creating new, useful or imaginative solutions. Students:

    a. know and use a deliberate design process for generating ideas, testing theories, creating innovative artifacts or solving authentic problems.

    b. select and use digital tools to plan and manage a design process that considers design constraints and calculated risks.

    c. develop, test and refine prototypes as part of a cyclical design process.

d. exhibit a tolerance for ambiguity, perseverance and the capacity to work with open-ended problems.

5. Computational Thinker

Students develop and employ strategies for understanding and solving problems in ways that leverage the power of technological methods to develop and test solutions. Students:

a. formulate problem definitions suited for technology-assisted methods such as data analysis, abstract models and algorithmic thinking in exploring and finding solutions.

b. collect data or identify relevant data sets, use digital tools to analyze them, and represent data in various ways to facilitate problem-solving and decision-making.

c. break problems into component parts, extract key information, and develop descriptive models to understand complex systems or facilitate problem-solving.

d. understand how automation works and use algorithmic thinking to develop a sequence of steps to create and test automated solutions.

6. Creative Communicator

Students communicate clearly and express themselves creatively for a variety of purposes using the platforms, tools, styles, formats and digital media appropriate to their goals. Students:

a. choose the appropriate platforms and tools for meeting the desired objectives of their creation or communication.

b. create original works or responsibly repurpose or remix digital resources into new creations.

c. communicate complex ideas clearly and effectively by creating or using a variety of digital objects such as visualizations, models or simulations.

d. publish or present content that customizes the message and medium for their intended audiences.

7. Global Collaborator

Students use digital tools to broaden their perspectives and enrich their learning by collaborating with others and working effectively in teams locally and globally. Students:

a. use digital tools to connect with learners from a variety of backgrounds and cultures, engaging with them in ways that broaden mutual understanding and learning.

b. use collaborative technologies to work with others, including peers, experts or community members, to examine issues and problems from multiple viewpoints.

c. contribute constructively to project teams, assuming various roles and responsibilities to work effectively toward a common goal.

d. explore local and global issues and use collaborative technologies to work with others to investigate solutions.

ISTE Standards for Educators

The ISTE Standards for Educators are your road map to helping students become empowered learners. These standards will deepen your practice, promote collaboration with peers, challenge you to rethink traditional approaches and prepare students to drive their own learning.

Empowered Professional

1. Learner

Educators continually improve their practice by learning from and with others and exploring proven and promising practices that leverage technology to improve student learning. Educators:

a. Set professional learning goals to explore and apply pedagogical approaches made possible by technology and reflect on their effectiveness.

b. Pursue professional interests by creating and actively participating in local and global learning networks.

    c. Stay current with research that supports improved student learning outcomes, including findings from the learning sciences.

2. Leader

Educators seek out opportunities for leadership to support student empowerment and success and to improve teaching and learning. Educators:

    a. Shape, advance and accelerate a shared vision for empowered learning with technology by engaging with education stakeholders.

    b. Advocate for equitable access to educational technology, digital content and learning opportunities to meet the diverse needs of all students.

    c. Model for colleagues the identification, exploration, evaluation, curation and adoption of new digital resources and tools for learning.

3. Citizen

Educators inspire students to positively contribute to and responsibly participate in the digital world. Educators:

    a. Create experiences for learners to make positive, socially responsible contributions and exhibit empathetic behavior online that build relationships and community.

    b. Establish a learning culture that promotes curiosity and critical examination of online resources and fosters digital literacy and media fluency.

    c. Mentor students in safe, legal and ethical practices with digital tools and the protection of intellectual rights and property.

    d. Model and promote management of personal data and digital identity and protect student data privacy.

Learning Catalyst

4. Collaborator

Educators dedicate time to collaborate with both colleagues and students to improve practice, discover and share resources and ideas, and solve problems. Educators:

    a. Dedicate planning time to collaborate with colleagues to create authentic learning experiences that leverage technology.

    b. Collaborate and co-learn with students to discover and use new digital resources and diagnose and troubleshoot technology issues.

    c. Use collaborative tools to expand students' authentic, real-world learning experiences by engaging virtually with experts, teams and students, locally and globally.

    d. Demonstrate cultural competency when communicating with students, parents and colleagues and interact with them as co-collaborators in student learning.

5. Designer

Educators design authentic, learner-driven activities and environments that recognize and accommodate learner variability. Educators:

Use technology to create, adapt and personalize learning experiences that foster independent learning and accommodate learner differences and needs.

Design authentic learning activities that align with content area standards and use digital tools and resources to maximize active, deep learning.

Explore and apply instructional design principles to create innovative digital learning environments that engage and support learning.

6. Facilitator

Educators facilitate learning with technology to support student achievement of the 2016 ISTE Standards for Students. Educators:

    a. Foster a culture where students take ownership of their learning goals and outcomes in both independent and group settings.

    b. Manage the use of technology and student learning strategies in digital platforms, virtual environments, hands-on makerspaces or in the field.

    c. Create learning opportunities that challenge students to use a design process and computational thinking to innovate and solve problems.

    d. Model and nurture creativity and creative expression to communicate ideas, knowledge or connections.

7. Analyst

Educators understand and use data to drive their instruction and support students in achieving their learning goals. Educators:

a. Provide alternative ways for students to demonstrate competency and reflect on their learning using technology.

b. Use technology to design and implement a variety of formative and summative assessments that accommodate learner needs, provide timely feedback to students and inform instruction.

c. Use assessment data to guide progress and communicate with students, parents and education stakeholders to build student self-direction.

INDEX

Numbers

K

L

M

N

U

U.S. Department of Education's Office of Educational
      Technology, 50, 58
Use and connect mathematical representations, 75

V

videos, showing, 51, 78
visual models, using, 26
visual presentations, 75
Vygotsky, L., 32, 76

W

Weintrop et al., 94
White, T., 41
Wiliam, D., 59
Wing, J., 94

Y

You do, We do, I do model, 7

Z

Zbiek, R. & Hollebrands, K., 95

Your Opinion Matters
Tell Us How We're Doing!

Your feedback helps ISTE create the best possible resources for teaching and learning in the digital age. Share your thoughts with the community or tell us how we're doing!

You Can:

- Write a review at amazon.com or barnesandnoble.com.

- Mention this book on social media and follow ISTE on Twitter @iste, Facebook @ISTEconnects or Instagram @isteconnects

- Email us at books@iste.org with your questions or comments.